ALSO BY EMMA TENNANT

The Bad Sister

Two Women of London:
The Strange Case of Ms. Jekyll and Mrs. Hyde

Faustine

Strangers: A Family Romance

Pemberley

Girlitude

Burnt Diaries

Sylvia and Ted

A House in Corfu

a house in
CORFU

A Family's Sojourn in Greece

EMMA TENNANT

A JOHN MACRAE BOOK
Henry Holt and Company

Henry Holt and Company, LLC
Publishers since 1866
115 West 18th Street
New York, New York 10011

Henry Holt ® is a registered trademark
of Henry Holt and Company, LLC.

Originally published in Great Britain in 2001
by Jonathan Cape, London.

Library of Congress Cataloging-in-Publication Data
ISBN: 0-8050-6897-X

Henry Holt Books are available for special
promotions and premiums. For details contact:
Director, Special Markets.

First American Edition 2002

Designed by Paula Russell Szafranski

Printed in the United States of America

1 3 5 7 9 10 8 6 4 2

For my mother Elizabeth,
my sister Catherine
and for Tim

A House in Corfu

W here are you planting this? Is it *xorta*—weed?'
And the old woman laughs up at me, whipping
her donkey on down the rocky path ahead before I have
time to answer. I hear her call her greeting to the many—
and invisible—other occupants of the Greek landscape:
'*Herete!*' as she wends her way to the sea from her tiny
demesne of olive and scrub. Her upright figure in black is
like a needle, threading through a patchwork of fiercely
owned and tended land that is as intimately known and
impossible to ignore as the network of interrelated families
in the village of Liapades, above us on the steep hill. All
those who call back are owners, brothers, uncles, daughters,
grandmothers and great-grandmothers of the land. And

here, for the past thirty-five years or more, since my parents bought squares and triangles of this Mediterranean quilt, we have been a part of the landscape too.

What I am carrying is actually a pot of mint, a present for my mother and for the garden she has made under the house on the old terraces that go down to the grove. I'm hoping the mint will join the landscape; surprisingly, given the curly-leafed basil, plentiful chives and small forests of wild thyme, rosemary and sage that guard the flights of stone steps to the bay, there has never been mint here at Rovinia. Everything else is here, one might say. The hill across the narrow valley from our house is covered with one of the few remaining examples of autochthonous wood remaining on the island, a tangle of holm-oak, myrtle, white Mediterranean heath, viburnum, bay, laurel, arbutus and Judas tree; beyond, on the mountains above the Plain of Liapades, every herb of the eastern Mediterranean seems to grow, giving off a summery smell that is both healing and soporific. But neither sign nor scent exists of the iridescent green that proclaims the presence of mint. Of course, I know it's lack of water that deprives us of that sharp taste in the *tsatsiki*, the local yoghurt mixed with sturdy cucumber from allotments up by the church; and of an unashamedly English mint sauce to go with the shoulder of lamb. It's what you forget, when you walk in the Tuscan lushness of this hidden, untouched land on the west coast of the island of Corfu. Cypresses stand firmly Italian against a Quattro-cento sky. Tiles on the roofs of the old houses left behind in the village in the scramble down to the sea are Venetian; crumbling, ochre and sun-baked to brown. It's only too easy to forget, when winter rain is plentiful, the long season of drought. When it comes to comparisons with Italy, the island of Corfu lies across the Ionian Sea from the heel of the country, Calabria, a long way south of Tuscany. Can I really expect my pot of mint to take, in these conditions? Am I trying to do the equivalent of growing strawberries at the North Pole?

Time has a way of eliding here, making a constantly changing pattern of lives and beliefs, light and sombre against the background of an ever-changing sea.

How did we come to be here? Could it really be that a cruise round the Greek islands—a cruise run by Swan Hellenic, with on-board lectures by archaeologists and historians, stop-overs at little-known ports, and the sense of adventure and excitement of the trip—had so enthused my (by then) late middle-aged parents that they decided there and then to throw over everything and live in Corfu? And I? How did I come to be drawn to this place, after my first glimpse down the wooded valley when playing truant on a trip for a glossy magazine, insisting that a group of hot journalists come with me over a boulder-strewn hillside to make a first long appraisal of the spot? Did I sense I was part of a chain, going back millennia to the first inhabitants of a slice of this beautiful coast? Was it a feeling that, despite the Venetian name, 'Rovinia'—meaning (gloomily) ruin, and causing friends to raise eyebrows and throw hands in the air when news broke of the plan to live in Corfu—there had been a great deal more in distant days than the crumbling lime-kiln along the path from the high-water mark and the traces of grey stone on abandoned cultivated land, long ago swallowed by the Mediterranean jungle on the hill? How did the site of the house my father would build, fifty yards above the bay, come to be decided on with such uncanny prescience?

For, as we sit here now, on the stone terrace above the bay, we realise, for the hundredth time, that the choice of site was extraordinary indeed. It's the autumn equinox, 21st September, and the mountain across the sea that unfurls before us—we call the mountain the Monkey's Head, for it is round and brown and intelligent-looking, and guards the entrance to the famous bay of Paleocastritsa—now wears an unusual piece of headgear. It is 7 p.m. and the red sun sets midway over the Monkey's Head—just above, in fact, a parting, a limestone scar, which runs down the centre of the skull. Far below, on rocks where foam shoots up, a white peacock's tail in the backlash of a southerly gale far out to sea, the light from the lighthouse will flash off and on, warning the ships of danger once darkness comes down.

Not now, though: not yet. This is a moment we savour each year at the spring and autumn equinoxes, the few seconds when the sun sinks into the ape's cranium, dead-centre, and we see not the face of a monkey but of a god. We know in those brief moments that the house we have built is, by an inexplicable coincidence, straight in the path of the sun. The sun is, invariably, red as blood when it disappears on those two equinoctial occasions—and, despite all the scepticism and sophistication of our age, we can't help shivering at the thought of sacrifice and ritual, of Greek tragedy and rebirth, and of the secrets that lie buried in the groves and on the shifting stony and sandy beaches of the bay.

Then it's suddenly dark. Scarlet feathers, all that remain of the monkey's hat, stream out across a sky washed with clouds of black and indigo. We're holding our drinks, a little embarrassed perhaps by the sense of having been plunged into the ancient world and then pulled from it again—and we turn to each other, and to the lighted sitting room beyond the verandah. Someone brings out whisky, and ice; and in a twilight going so fast it's barely possible to see the terracotta pot where the mint grows, on the balustrade above the trees and shrubs on the hillside, I pick a sprig and add it to a drink. Yes, the mint has accepted its new home, on the west coast of the island of Corfu. But it will only live here if tended like a precious plant; it refuses to spread and naturalise. And now, as I look down in dusk at the rings and rusty covers of the seven wells we dug when we first came here to live, I wonder that I ever thought this water-craving herb would settle down with us at all.

*It's a hot day, and the sun comes in through the long, dusty win-*dows of the estate agent's office and makes a ring of rainbow bubbles around the surface of the tiny cups of *metriou* coffee on the desk between us. It's an indispensable part of the negotiations, which Pandelios's black-skirted, white-bloused young secretary seems to serve with the same air of solicitude that I remember at a monastery on the pinnacles of Meteora: a thimble of coffee; a *loukoumi*, pale rose-water Turkish delight powdered with fine sugar; a tall glass and a short one, with water and ouzo respectively. She could be the daughter of the *papas* I still see in my mind's eye when, with a friend (and refusing the offer of being hauled up in a basket to the summit), we had climbed the hundreds of steps and entered the dark, incense-haunted church and gone through into the high, vaulted library. With her dark eyes and downcast expression, she could be an icon, a Byzantine Madonna captured in a painted haze of gold sunshine. But before I can romanticise any further, Pandelios the estate agent has stretched across me to hand the little white china cups to my mother and father, and the conversation continues where it had broken off with the arrival of the sweet, thick *metriou*.

'Anna Georgiadis is holding out for more,' Pandelios says. His bushy hair, reddish and receding at the temples, makes him look like a pantomime lion. 'It's a vital part of the property, as you know, so I'm afraid you'll have to take her terms.'

'Very well,' comes my father's answer. 'We don't want anyone to be unhappy there—and her parcel of land does lie right in the middle of the grove. As we said before, we want the right of way down from the village to continue—in fact we wouldn't dream of stopping anyone from bringing their sheep down to graze anywhere on the land'—and he turns to my mother, who nods in confirmation. 'The only way the fishermen can get down to the sea is by going on the path just behind the house we plan to build,' my father goes on. 'And we wouldn't contemplate blocking the path when we own those *stremata* [acres] at the top of the hill.'

Pandelios scratches his chin and looks business-like, but

I can tell he is pleased with our wish to leave undisturbed the way of life of the Corfiots in this remote part of the west coast. There have been stories—we are actually only to hear them later—of the foolhardy foreigner who blocked access to the well on his land, only to find the well blocked up with cement the next time he came to the island to enjoy his property. And stories of hauntings, of the patron saint, St Spiridon, displeased at an incomer's reluctance to share amenities that have belonged to the local people for as long as there has been a St Spiridon in the great gold catafalque in the town's church. But at the time of our meeting with the estate agent, we knew none of this. We just knew it didn't make sense to demand privacy when the seashore belongs to everyone—and is anyway never short of men pushing out their boats or dragging them up the beach again. The landscape, however empty it may look, has as many denizens as a tapestry depicting hidden animals in a forest alive with huntsmen and spears. In Greece, you're never alone, and when I put in my contribution—saying the word for private is *idiotikos*, and surely there must be a good reason for that—everyone laughs, though the agent and his demure secretary laugh a trifle uncertainly. Will we really leave the local population to their old ways, which involve a 4 a.m. trudge down the rock path and on to the shingle, shouting as the boats are rolled out over logs, voices echoing across the water and ricocheting back to the valley we are about to buy? Do we know what we're letting ourselves in for? Smart folk from Athens would be likely to try and restrict the ways and livelihoods of country and fishing people by building private marinas and swimming pools.

Why not us? 'I don't want a fence at the high-tide mark where the beach goes into the grove,' my mother says when Pandelios makes a suggestion that public and private land should be separated by the erection of boards and notices. 'It should all flow—one into the other, not shut off at all.' And the agent looks in amazement and relief at these two *xenoi*, the foreigners who want all to make use of the land near the sea below Liapades.

Of course, that was then. As I daydream (for I'm not involved in the financial side of this new life-plan of my parents, and at the time—the early 1960s—I had no idea how strong a part the place would play in my own life), I look out of the window on a typical street scene of Corfu town. Tall Venetian houses, in faded watermelon colours, lean like guests at a party, slightly jaded by their long years of civilised enjoyment. The street is narrow, and a woman walks along with a bag of small artichokes and a carrier bursting with minute fish, a kind of whitebait it seems, which glint silver in the spring sunlight. I imagine it's her midday meal, for I know offices close at lunchtime and don't reopen until at least five in the evening, the afternoon idled away in the sacred Greek siesta. I see a table, a balcony, a blind pulled low, as it is already hot at this time of year by one o'clock. A dish is on the table, in a darkened room just inside from the balcony with its ornamental railing. Elegant and curved, this is in all probability a relic of the French occupation of Corfu. In the dish are small artichokes, to be eaten whole, with a side plate of minuscule broad beans, startlingly green due to the removal of the outer skin, the bean being gripped between finger and thumb.

'I will speak to Anna Georgiadis and explain she may also bring her goats to the grove,' says Pandelios, while I feel my parents control their reaction to the prospect: sheep add to the charming rural idyll under the olives, but *goats?* 'So, unless there are any problems, I believe we have discussed all there is to discuss,' Pandelios concludes. (Of course there will be problems. But, for now, we pretend all is well.) Pandelios glances out of the window, and I see in his eyes the pleasure of anticipating the coming meal. I hope for him that he will have the new season's artichokes, so tender the inner thistle doesn't need to be cut out. And I find myself wishing now for a *frittura* of the little fish.

'We'll have lunch at the harbour, shall we?' my parents say, after we have said goodbye to Pandelios and arranged to meet again next week, to explore the necessity for a foreign company to be formed in order to buy land in Corfu. I agree, and accompany them, as entranced by this new direction in all our lives as they so clearly are. But before we go I listen to Pandelios's last story—about the tradition of the youngest son of a Greek family inevitably being the recipient of the poorest land as his inheritance: shallow and gravel-choked, with brackish water, away from the good agricultural areas and near the sea. 'Yet this may all change for the youngest sons,' Pandelios says, as if recounting a fairy-tale that he senses is destined for a new ending. 'When people come who want to live by the sea,' he says thoughtfully, looking at us, an English family with no apparent need to uproot and come to live in Corfu, 'then, I think, all may very well change.' And he smiles and waves to us, and we walk down the street. I hadn't liked to ask, in the halting demotic I had learnt a couple of years before, whether our good agent was himself the youngest son in his family.

The island of Corfu is sixty miles long and thirty miles wide at its widest. The mountains—particularly Pantokrator with its Olympian splendour—give an illusion of scale to the island that is quite at odds with the reality. Corfu looks out at Albanian mountains to the east, and across the sea to Italy in the west, with mountain ranges, again, giving the sense of a land of limitless proportions. Giants or trolls must once have lived here, one thinks when morning makes of the mountains a blue-mauve hugeness along the edges of the plain between Liapades and the eastern side of the island, the Plain of Ropa; or when evening pencils the mountains black, as if they had turned to sleeping giants themselves. Space, as well as time, is unreliable here: the prevalence of mountains makes for winding roads, corkscrews that draw the clear air like wine from the necks of valleys and gorges as one goes up and up, and then drops down. It can take longer to travel five miles, in Corfu, than to drive across a prairie or an entire county in England—the Somerset Levels, say, or the East Anglian fens.

So what are the size and scale of the land we have bought, in this land of endless miles and long-distance journeys to the nearest mountain village? How do we measure the depth and width of Rovinia, how do we throw in the unchartable sea? Will we feel cramped or generously accommodated in our new home? Will we have the sense of perching on a ledge, if we hack out rock from the hillside and build there—or will it seem as if the house has always been waiting for us to build it, just as wide and long as it was intended by nature to be?

The most difficult problems, it seems, are these. However meticulous the plan, the finished living space may somehow just be wrong. The landscape has refused you; and the mountains across the big bay at Paleocastritsa, which can disappear into a roof of cloud and rain, will frown across the water at efforts unrewarded by 'rightness' of scale and measurement. It's a responsibility I can see weighs heavily on my father, who is enough of an architect to have built a Georgian doll's house of exquisite proportions for me as a child, a yacht (for my brother) and a Gothic castle for my younger sister. He'll try none of these here in Corfu, obviously; but what exactly *is* 'right', in this island where the Venetians were succeeded by the French, at the time of the Revolution, and then the French by the British, just as the most deadly Victorian architecture was becoming fashionable? He won't build good Queen Victoria's Osborne on this Mediterranean shore, complete with ramparts to enable John Brown to look out across the sea. He won't be drawn to Italian *palazzi* or anything too grandly pretentious, that's for sure. But for now, as we make the lengthy trip—the road in those early days across the island has more potholes than the worst of its kind in Ireland or Scotland—we have no ideas about the future appearance of the house at Rovinia. And if he does, he's not letting on.

So what do we own? Or, if Anna Georgiadis consents to sell her strip of land in the grove, what will we own, once the hideous complications of buying land on a Greek island that is a 'borderline' area (in the case of Corfu, a mere mile across Corfu channel to Albania) have been resolved? Is our terrain large or small, confined by steep hills or a wide passageway to the sea? It depends on how you look at it, you could say: to us, as we finally drive down the side road to Liapades and park the car in the *plateia* between the church and the *cafeneon* where the old men sit staring at us tortoise-like in the evening sun, it is clearly a place that has always been there, a place of significance once, though when and how we shall probably never know. We haven't just decided to set ourselves down on raw, uncultivated woodland, to hack away at the ground and make a new place to live. We're *returning*: that's the unmistakable feeling we get, even in these days when we hardly know the land below Liapades by the edge of the sea. And there's just time, before the sun sets, to go at a brisk pace down the boulder-strewn path—twenty minutes down, twenty-five back up—before the sun sets and a primeval darkness seizes land and Liapades alike.

A *monopati*—a Greek path, that most essential of travel methods of much of Greece in those days, and to this day the only way to go down the length of the roadless west coast from Rovinia to the south of the island—has its quota of obstacles, and we walk warily past the mad white dog (which once chewed off the end of the stick I was carrying). People—always people—inhabit here, and just when you think you're unobserved, alone in this Arcadian paradise, the oddest of the villagers comes at you: the ancient crone who clutches my mother's sleeve and wants her question answered, with the urgency of a seeker after the truth of the Sphinx—but none of us can understand the question. The boy, staring-eyed and jowly, who in the past would have been known as the village idiot in England: he lopes along behind us, until he loses patience and wanders off back up the hill again. The donkey, tethered to a stake at the side of the path, which aims a kick and gives a long, mournful bray at the same time (its owner, previously invisible in the woods, appears in her black clothes to tie bundles of faggots to its back). The birds, jay and golden oriole—and, as we grow nearer the sea, white gulls, circling and diving, always going back to the carpet of blue that spreads out in the gaps between the cypress and olive trees.

Forty-two *stremata* (about twelve acres) of all this are shortly to be ours.

*It wasn't long before we discovered that Rovinia—land over-*grown except for, here and there, a small vegetable patch in the deep incline at the end of the valley; or, in the case of the sweep down to the sea, grazed and olive-picked, clearly a part of the jigsaw of Liapades owners—was very probably just where Homer had placed the famous meeting between the shipwrecked and naked Odysseus and the princess, Nausicaa. As anyone fortunate enough to find themselves in these acres—where the west wind blows day and night and the sea turns violent blue, crude as a child's paintbox colour, when it swings to the *maestro* (surely the wind that brought Odysseus's boat on the rocks)—will know, there must be literally hundreds of origins for this chapter in the *Odyssey*. Isn't there a scholarly book, anyway, which 'proves' that the historic encounter took place in Sicily? Yet the evidence, as we come to piece it together in the summer of the house being built, does appear to conclude that it really was in 'our' bay, on 'our' beach and in the grove where Anna Georgiadis now frolics with her goats. Rovinia was the scene of the most romantic non-romance of the antique world.

We're sitting at a table, late lunchtime, in (at this time, 1965) the only hotel for miles and discussing the evidence from our different points of view.

'There, after all, is the ship,' says my father, prepared to suspend disbelief on so warm and agreeable a day, when retsina is brought to the table by boys running like deer and *xoriatiki* salad, as they make it in the village, comes down before us in big shared bowls. He spears a lump of feta, looks less happily at an olive, then overcomes the dislike of a lifetime and pops it in his mouth. He smiles; as long as there's no mention of garlic, he will eat the food at the Tourist Pavilion happily.

'Yes,' agrees Peter, a young actor friend of mine. He is less contented than the rest of us: the Tourist Pavilion—situated in Corfu's most renowned and beautiful bay of Paleocastritsa, and enjoying a position on a piece of land that turns, magically, to beach and then to a wooded isthmus, which joins it with the next inlet of blue water on the coast—has rooms for all of us, but no room for Peter. Another, much smaller hotel has just been completed, about a hundred yards back from the view that Edward Lear, watercolourist and nonsense poet, painted so often: delicate, exact portrayals of the bay and the steep hill at its western tip, where the monastery stands high and white. The new, less view-blessed hotel has daringly been named The Living Lobster.

Peter has to share with a dentist, who snores. 'I might join Odysseus's ship,' he jokes. 'At least I might get a cabin to myself.'

The boat is ineluctably there, out in the wide stretch of water beyond Paleocastritsa bay, making what seems at first to be a great lake, guarded by the Monkey's Head with its flashing beacon on one side, and by the curve of the coastline as it plunges south on the other. In the middle, three bays to the south of where we sit, and just the right distance from the rock everyone claims is Odysseus's boat, turned to stone by the gods after it foundered in heavy seas, is Rovinia Bay.

'Odysseus could easily swim to our beach from there,' says my younger sister Catherine, who is seventeen and so obsessed with the sea that she swims with my mother right down the virgin coast to the south of us, clambering out from time to time to lie like a seal on the beaches at Yalli and Iliodoros. 'And then there was the river, where he could wash off all the salt on his back.'

We all fall silent, realising Catherine's schooling has been more recent than ours. But the image of the handsome young man's salt-encrusted back returns, followed by a conversation, increasingly argumentative, on the subject of the riverbed at Rovinia. It is dried-out now, bearer of Judas trees with their bright purple blossoms in spring, and wild quinces and pear. But water is known to rush down in sudden torrents, as if a plug has been let out somewhere up the high hill under Liapades, when the winter rains force the riverbed to revert to river. Then, so we've been told, the water rushes out on to the beach, sculpting new sandbanks, covering the shingle and turning the blue sea to a muddy brown. 'Of course it must have been a river in Homeric times,' says Mark, a friend whose cousin, a dauntingly well-educated cosmopolitan, occupies a house on the east of the island, above Corfu town. 'And Lawrence Durrell states that Homer identifies the bay where Odysseus swam ashore from the wreck as three bays south of Paleocastritsa, which was certainly where King Alcinous, the father of Nausicaa, had his palace. This proves it, surely.'

Fish comes to the table at last, and we all watch as my father, host to this party of his children and their friends, fillets it carefully: *sinegrida*, a large and succulent fish not unlike a *loup de mer*; and *barbouni*, red mullet sharp and tangy, and delicious with lemon and olive oil. Plates of chips—the eternal Greek chips—join the salad with its shredded lettuce and carrot, feta, olives and onion and cucumber. The retsina, so strong you can actually feel under attack from an entire pine forest, slips gold into our tumblers. '*Ighia!*'—health!—we say, if a trifle self-consciously.

It is late afternoon by the time we step into the little boat that will take us over the sea from Paleocastritsa to the bay where the foundations of our new house have been laid on the hillside.

The engine of the little fishing caique is uncertain, and midway there we simply stop and sit in the great silence of the distant mountains and the soft whisper of the sea.

This is what it must have been like, I think, when the storm blew away and Odysseus stood on the beach and looked back at his petrified ship under a clear sky. It was like this then.

But before I have time to summon up the picture of King Alcinous's palace—with its bronze walls and great terrace, its four acres of garden with peach and vine, left behind us on the slopes above Paleocastritsa Bay—the engine, responding to a pull on the string from Yannis the fisherman, gives an ear-splitting roar. We lurch forward, over water so clear that we can see small fish down by the white stones on the seabed at least forty feet below. A flying fish leaps from the calm inlet by the mouth of the cave on the southern side of the bay. We seem to dash at the shingle as if we, too, are trying to fly over the sea. There is no time at all to return in time: to think of the tabloid story that the meeting of Odysseus and the daughter of the king from Paleocastritsa would make today. The princess and the naked stranger who comes ashore; her revelations to her confidantes that this man could be a husband for her. The invitation to the palace and the journey there, in the great wagon, over ancient cobbled roads along to Lakones and then down the grove of Athena to the palace, where Alcinous and Arete live happily ever after . . .

We have to jump out of the boat into the sea. Yannis says tomorrow will be *asximos kairos*, bad weather, and not a good day for a trip down the coast with a picnic. '*Metavrio*,' the day after tomorrow, he insists, as we stand on the shingle, dazed after our long meal, staring up at the beginnings of a new life—for my parents, at least. I wish them all the happiness of the King and Queen, in their three-and-a-half-thousand-years-ago lives at Paleocastritsa. And I walk up the dried-out riverbed, where in this high summer heat there are still poppies growing amongst the stones. Then, with

Peter and Mark and my sister, I walk up the olive grove that runs beside the river: surely this wide grove has always been here; surely this is where Nausicaa and Odysseus met and talked?

'*Katzikaki, katzikako*,' comes a screeching voice at the end of the grove where the olives go up in wide terraces to the tangle of scrub and trees on the hill. '*Ela, ela . . . !*'

The goats stand in the grove, baring their teeth and moving deftly to the middle of the brown carpeting of olive leaves and pine needles that have replaced the green of earlier months. They're getting ready to kick, and they look as if they mean to do it hard.

'*Katzikaki*,' comes the ugly jay sound again. Then an old woman, so wrapped in black that her face and limbs are barely visible, darts down through the trees. '*Kali spera!*' she screams at us, and thus moves the long day into evening, as the Greek greetings invariably do. With one hand she tugs at a leash hidden in the leaves scattered on the floor of the grove, and we see to our further shame that the goats were tethered to the olive trees all along.

This was my first glimpse of Anna Georgiadis.

Collas is the name of the architect who has sited our house. His wife Maria is a grand island lady who doesn't come down the precipice to observe her husband's deliberations. I meet her once—and, despite her pleasant smile and smart town suit, I feel we are all a million miles from her, in attitude and in the way we appreciate this (to her) distinctly too out-of-the-way spot. She's a Corfiot, and we are not; but I've seen enough of the country people round here to know how much easier they are to get on with than the Greek middle class. They ask direct questions, of course, the fisherfolk, and sometimes of the crudest nature—but the Athenian, or Corfu-bourgeois is just as eager to know how much money you have, whether you sleep with your husband/wife, how old you are; and their way of asking tends to be masked by a false good nature. One of the joys of this remote spot, I soon understand, is that it doesn't attract the wearer of court shoes, the carrier of handbags. The path must be taken seriously; and I hear my father, as he paces the land where the walls of Rovinia House will go up, speaking against applying for a road to lead to the property.

To the north of the land that will comprise Rovinia is a steeply shelving set of terraces, these facing out to a landscape so unlike the Homeric grove and wooded hill we have come to see as the most beautiful of the island's bays that it could appear to belong to another country. The cliffs across a small, perfect—but sunless—bay are pink and grey, huge and rugged, a kind of Albania of the imagination. Edward Lear painted and portrayed in watercolour the wildness and roughness of this scene so near to us and yet so distant; and my father soon sketches and paints this operatic scenery.

Yet the possibility of houses going up on these terraces is far from agreeable. We can all see in our mind's eye the steps hewn in rock leading down to the sea, to a platform of rock and a sunny raft out in the water; and my parents, who dread noise at night (and we will come to live with it for several summers, from music floating with the power of sound-over-water across the large bay to us from Paleocastritsa) become determined to ensure a calm and silence that only privacy can bring. The land must be bought, in this outpost of Rovinia: beyond the house is the high hump of the hill; then the *monopati*, which must be left open to the fisherfolk; then the *stremata* that go down to the edge of the precipice where (already) a rectangular cement box has been constructed, this the weekend cottage (so we assume) of a dweller in Corfu town. Noise from the cement box won't affect us, as the position is low on the cliff edge (it's a temptation to push it over), but higher up a development of houses would certainly be audible. So, with the same long pauses, acceptances and withdrawals, these pretty, sun-bathed terraces are bought; and it's impossible not to think they're a safeguard, too, against a future decision to sell or leave Rovinia. Even with that gone, this cliff garden of scrub and olive facing a majestic ravine will still belong to us.

'But will you not find it difficult here in winter or when the sea is rough and you cannot go round to Alipa [the nearest harbour] by boat?' asks Collas. He is too polite to speak out against my father's wishes, but he looks incredulous. Tall, pale, with the air of an intellectual, our architect has yet to draw up plans for the English, and the way in which my parents are intending to isolate themselves clearly alarms him. Do they know how grim it can be here right through the winter downpours and storms, cold and windy right up to *Pasca*, the Greek Easter that is the watershed of the year, whenever it falls in the calendar? Then I see his brow—as pale as only a Greek office-dweller's can be, who avoids the national glory, the sun—crease further. He steals a glance at us as we stand on the floor of the room where we will one day sit, eat and watch the swallows make their long calls as they fly back and forth from the verandah outside. Are we perhaps in trouble? In dire financial straits? Are we hiding from the police, even, with our stated desire not to apply for a road? 'Of course, the land up to the village has so many owners,' Collas adds, trying to make sense of it all: he's seen the negotiations, the withdrawals and retracted acceptances of the six who own the pieces of land that form the 'estate' of Rovinia. Not to mention the troubles and demands of Anna Georgiadis, his sympathetic glance seems to say. Little wonder the very idea of making a road doesn't appeal. 'And it would be very expensive,' Collas ends up, diplomatically.

The reaction of the architect to my father's firm rejection of a link with the outside world does, however, lead me to ponder what is being given up and what embraced, in this unexpected move to an island never visited until the occasion of an island cruise a few years back. What had they thought, my parents, when, on deciding to return to Corfu a year after their first vision of the west coast, they found themselves in a small boat, being rowed over from Paleocastritsa to the secret bay at Rovinia—secret because no-one had 'discovered' it yet, and only fishermen frequented the shore? Had they taken into account the challenge that building in so inaccessible a spot would be? Had they decided, there and then, to give up a home in England (or Scotland, as happened to be the case) and settle permanently in the valley by the sea?

As I was to discover years later, the decision to live

permanently in Corfu didn't come as a bolt from the Ionian blue. The house was planned as a substitute for the modest farmhouse in the South of France they'd sold in the mid 1960s—a holiday house that could also be let out. It was only in the summer of 1964, while sitting on the neighbouring beach of Stellari and staring out to sea from the great expanse of sand there, that the decision was reached to live at Rovinia all year round. My father, then aged sixty-five and two years from leaving his City job, had a 'why not?' attitude when the idea struck them both simultaneously; the rest is Rovinia's myth and history.

And it doesn't need saying that anyone wanting to up sticks and move a thousand miles, to a country where a foreign language is spoken and the local customs are in need of strict observance, must be so filled with wonder by the place that they are, like Odysseus as he approaches Circe's island, incapable of stopping themselves from anchoring there.

It wasn't hard to see that this valley three bays south of Paleocastritsa had everything.

The cave on the southern extremity of the bay was claimed by some to be Prospero's (but, unlike the ship overturned by waves as it came into view of the Phaeacians, there is no real evidence for this. Unless the *Odyssey* can be counted as evidence, that is—and why not?). But, even had it not been Prospero's, this was clearly an extraordinary cave. To find, as we did soon after moving there, that a path runs up inside this almost artificial-looking entrance to the Underworld (the proportions are so perfect one half-expects an eighteenth-century party on the Grand Tour to stroll from its delectable grey, black and white mouth) made the cave even more mysterious than before. Where did this path lead? Whom did it serve, so steep and dark, before coming out on to a brambly path, the only way down the coast along the high cliffs? Smugglers, perhaps? Sailors fleeing from the black storm behind them in a raging sea?

The grove was equally enticing: so gracious, wide and prettily flanked by olive trees in their prime. I felt the first time I went there the odd silence that comes down as soon as one walks along the grove towards the woods that go up the hill. It's a place that is both inland and sea-guarded; where the waves come in like the white net skirts of ballerinas, green silk at their back, and just a few paces away from the shore is the interior.

Little wonder, then, that my parents made an instant decision when they stepped from the rowing-boat and stood by the cave and the olive grove and the sea. It didn't seem like a decision, probably—like all the best decisions.

But now, as we turn to Collas the architect in the hope of reassuring him of our sanity, we find it is his turn to demonstrate (though of course we don't recognise this at the time) that he lives in another world to that of the sensible, the wise. 'Oh yes, you will find water without much difficulty here,' Collas says. He glances at his watch; evening in the colonnaded town awaits him. And tomorrow he comes here again, to supervise the building of the walls, which will be of limestone blasted from the quarry on the hill behind the property. 'You shouldn't have a problem finding water at all,' Collas says again, as he picks his way up through the rocks on the long haul back to the village.

It's a strange sensation, seeing the beginnings of a house where none has been dreamt of before. First—and it seemed an act of barbarism—the wood is cut by hand, at least ten men hacking and pulling at bushes and trees that seem to take on human proportions as they are dragged from the ground: an elderly satyr, in the tortured branches of an arbutus tree; nymphs struggling against the rape of the woodcutters, in their bright dresses. Do we really need to destroy so much ancient forest and scrub—and then blow a large portion of the rock beneath sky-high in order to enjoy a fine view and stroll on terraces still impossible to envisage? Are we *colons*, the new type, who pretend to blend in with the landscape and then, unstoppably, cut swathes through it, bulldozing and wrecking to the end?

At least there won't be bulldozers; and thus, no question of a road. The very thought of the mechanised dinosaurs trying to come down into this Paradise causes a shudder. Of course, it's not just bulldozers that the workmen have to do without—for what can't come down the *monopati* can't get here by sea either: no drills, no machinery that would make Nikiforos, brave Foreman of the diggers of Rovinia foundations, throw up his hands in relief. We are in an antique past here; and while we may enjoy dreaming of the *Iliad* and the *Odyssey* (or of neolithic ancestors: my father, after the first blasting of the rock, has already found some shards of what seems very old pottery: '*Ela*,' says Nikiforos, when he's proudly shown it—and he points at the crumbling and disused lime-kiln at the foot of the hill opposite: '*Ela* [Come], I show you!' and he skips across the valley at an amazing speed, to return with similar brown crockery, clearly no more than five years old).

Not that the diggers (there are twenty-eight of these altogether) seem unused to the primitive methods forced upon them here at Rovinia. We arrive each day at around 10 a.m. to watch the proceedings and to walk about in the *stremata* that we still find it hard to believe are ours to wander in. Sometimes I sit in the grove and read, feeling grateful for the shade of the olive trees as it grows deeper with the increasing power of the sun. All goes well at first, but soon, drawn by the incessant labour up the hill, I lay the book down—several novels by Elizabeth Bowen and the works of the Durrell brothers have been abandoned this way—but, as it doesn't rain all summer, they are regularly rescued, their pages slightly baked, from the earthen hollows where they were left at the foot of the trees. I go up the rough paths on the steep slope to the site of the house. And each time I am astonished by the energy of the men, picks in hand, as they dig deep to make the foundations. Sun makes stripes of sweat on their backs and the earth is eaten by their spiked blows. The base of the new building is almost there, thanks to the men from Lakones, the village so high on the mountain across the bay of Paleocastritsa that it is often invisible, in a dark-blue fog that looks as if it's been thrown there by an angry Zeus; and results, too, are due to the men of Doukades, and those from Liapades itself. Marsalas, one of the diggers, comes up to my mother on the last day of the digging of the foundations of Rovinia and hands her what looks like a corn dolly—though maybe the original material is reeds from the reedbeds by a hidden pond on the Plain of Ropa. This is a good sign: Nikiforos has ensured pleasant working conditions (as far as that's possible, in this blazing heat) and everyone laughs at my father's cheerful attempts to communicate without learning a word of Greek.

Now, a week later, the walls are going up. Each day when we come—by boat if the sea permits it, by road if it's rough (we stop always at the one gap in the hills where it's possible to look across at our bay and say 'There it is!', the shore white and crescent-moon shaped, protective cliffs holding it; the cave agape, waiting for our entry to its dark coolness)—each day the walls go higher and the house begins to look as if it will one day be ready for us to live in. Windowframes are ordered from Sotiri, the carpenter, and it's strange to think of these views envisaged by my father—he paces out the distances between them on the newly flattened rock, the future terrace—as one day framed by curtains and crowned with wooden poles.

There's a long way to go, of course. But the fact that the house is coming up vertically from the side of the hill—pale and ghostly, the rooms could be tombs, I can't help thinking morbidly, as the car rattles down over the potholes on the unmade road to Liapades—gives an indication of the efforts that have been made to get this far. There was a blasting of rock in the hill on the northern side of the valley, before the stone could be laid to build out and form a terrace that will run down the side of the house facing south. (The other side of the house is right up against the hill behind.) There will be space for a passage leading from a wood-store at the back; the passage will have a boiler room off it, and an area for drying clothes out of view of the kitchen. The terrace will be three yards wide, and at the western extremity there will be another place to sit—which I can tell already occupies my mother's thoughts as we clamber out of the hired car in the *plateia* in Liapades and begin the vertiginous descent on foot to Rovinia once more.

I can understand why this particular spot holds a place in my mother's heart before its future beauties can even be discerned. There's the quality of the natural rocky wall—cistus with its pink and white flowers grows down over it, and broom in spring, and rosemary and thyme grow wild in great bushes along the top of the wall, to make a stunning background for the plants she'll want to put in. This terrace will be the first thing a visitor sees when coming in to the sitting room. The sea, too: a long blue swirl straight from the tube marked Ultramarine. This sea-facing part of the house, with her bedroom directly above the long sitting room, has everything she must always have dreamt of: the Mediterranean (only in this case the Ionian Sea); the chance to grow a vine just under her bedroom, which will one day provide shade for eating out on the stone apron; the marriage of olive tree and shrub with cultivated flowers; even (thrown in for good luck) an oblique view of the famous cave.

As we come down the steepest part of the cliff above Rovinia, the part where the path simply gives up and runs off in several directions, like hair that has been prepared for plaiting and then abandoned, we stop for a moment and look down at the first view of the bay from above. The site of the house is clearly visible: the strawberry grapes my mother will grow along the iron framework over the far terrace clearly established in all our minds, as she tells us of the heady scent the little purple grapes give off, enhanced by sudden showers of September rain. 'Hibiscus', my mother is saying as we stand, staring down at what will be Rovinia House, '*Datura* . . .' And to a chorus of 'What's that?' she begins to explain: 'A great white drooping bell of a flower— terribly poisonous but very beautiful. And gardenias, as well as the lovely geranium that's there already, of course . . .'

'What about the low garden?' someone says. The speaker is Marie Aspioti, who in the space of a few short meetings has become a close friend on the island. Marie is from an old family fallen on hard times, lives with her mother in a large, dilapidated house in the town and is about as far from the 'smart' lady of Corfu as it is possible to get. Marie teaches English now, to earn a living, and her sister teaches folk dance (on my first visit to the island, when I led the hot journalists to inspect the site at Rovinia, I'd been staying in a castellated hotel to the north of the town, and after dinner there a wild, white-haired lady had shown the precision of the Greek dance steps with great aplomb and accuracy). Marie it is who has grown close to us—to these foreigners—but then she has all her life been a friend of Patrick Leigh Fermor, the author, amongst other extraordinary books, of *Mani*.

'I thought we might dig out a sunken garden right at the lowest point of the land,' my mother says rather shyly. Although she has a natural affinity with gardens and with plants in the wild, she resists the label of expert or even practised gardener.

'It is a good idea,' Marie pronounces, her elfish face breaking into a smile. She is small, with a determined walk, and even in the height of summer wears brown sweater and jacket and tweed skirt: she is an Anglophile, living in her imagination in an England where this is the right costume all year round, and of course she may well be right. 'You have all those terraces that need repair,' Marie points out as we continue down a deep gorge where the path, having decided to reconstitute itself, plunges us without so much as a zigzag under scrub grown so tall it is as menacing as jungle. 'Then when they are built up again, you may set out flowerbeds on them.'

Neither my mother nor I say anything in reply, but I know we both feel that the crumbling terraces of grey stone that go down the hill behind the house now being built are on no account to be 'modernised' or restored. They'll have irises and plumbago and lemon trees growing on them— they already have the lemons, large and green and knobbly, ripening to an acidic yellow in the spring—and then, never to be omitted, wild flowers, for which this terraced (and pre- sumably once vine-cultivated) land will make a perfect base. We recite the names of the few we can positively look forward to identifying, once we're all back here (we hope) in the spring. 'Marigold, grape hyacinth, speedwell, scarlet pimpernel, anemone, star-of-Bethlehem, bee orchids, hon- esty . . .' Our voices tail off: Marie, who teaches us so much about Greece, and about the secrets of Corfu, adds to the list while we all fall uncharacteristically silent. 'Lithosper- mum,' she says, reminding us of the gentian-blue flower that loves to grow on a bank beside a leaking pipe, and we all start up again: 'Camomile, campanula . . .'

The litany goes on, as we complete the last tortuous

portion of the path and come down on the peninsula, a razor-backed fish of layered stone jutting out to sea, which is where we turn sharply to the left to arrive at Mr Collas and the site of Rovinia House.

We've arrived too early. The place is deserted, with an unappealing glare coming off the sea, and the half-built walls of the house could as well be a ruin as the start of an exciting new life.

Why didn't we guess the siesta would run until well after five in the afternoon? It does in the town, where the closed shops with their grilles pulled down and the empty Corfu Bar (there are so few tourists at this stage that the northerners, with their ignorance of the siesta, have not yet brought an unwanted life to the afternoons) don't fill up till the blue hour of evening. Do we expect the builders here to toil right through this great heat? Why shouldn't they lie in the dappled shade of the olives (and, as our eyes acclimatise to the glare, we see they are doing precisely that) and wait until a more civilised time for carrying stone and cement up to the site? The fact that every single one of the builders is a woman makes our air of dismay all the more unsuitable. After all, we couldn't take the weight—not even a half of the loads they carry—and we certainly couldn't, as they do, bring it up all fifty yards on our heads.

'*Sica!*' As always in the apparently empty landscape, a figure emerges, barely visible at first in the scrub on the side of the hill beneath our feet. The figure is a boy, about ten years old, and as soon as he reaches us and sets down a wide pannier on the just-laid terrace, he runs off again, this time to climb the tree we'd failed to see him in: a tall, majestic tree laden with dark fruit.

'Figs!' we all say together, as if we somehow knew this part of the afternoon demands the plunge into the interior of a fig: purple, scented, as intermeshed with scarlet and purple filaments as an Ottoman tapestry. A fig will quench thirst and satisfy hunger: most important of all, it will give a sense of languorous shade, away from a time of day that is too brassy and open, the sun hanging like a gold coin in a sky that's overdone it on the blue.

The child runs up again, his hands full. The figs have a green, soft skin like the leather slippers on sale in the market: easily bruised, yet resilient. We bite in, only my father thinking to ask how much we should give the boy for his efforts.

'*Decca drachmas*,' comes the boy's voice, as if he could understand us perfectly well.

'Nonsense!' Marie says in English. 'They're your figs anyway,' and she laughs at my father, to show the folly of his offer to pay. She then narrows her eyes, and looks just like the schoolmistress she is. '*Ela, paidi mou*,' Marie says, 'come here, child.' And we see her slip a tube of what looks suspiciously like cough sweets into his hand. '*Ti lei?*' she demands, as if coaching the child in the catechism.

The boy hangs his head. Although she doesn't come often to this side of the island, the chances are that Maria will know whose son this is; and that she will have attended his christening, departing with the sugared almonds and extravagant sweets that are deemed essential on these occasions. She may even be a *koumbara*, one of the many godparents of the child, calling out to the waiting children in the street the name they have all chosen for the just-baptised child. Sure enough, Marie does appear to know a good deal about the lad. 'Ten drachmas indeed,' she mutters as he darts off, clutching the cough sweets with an expression that can only be described as wry, resigned. 'Yannis is Dassia's boy,' Marie begins. 'Now there's a tale . . .'

Before she can go any further, the afternoon suddenly wakes up. Down in the grove a procession appears, religious perhaps, as the white head-dresses march slowly under the trees and turn to mount the path on our side of the hill. We stand, figs half in our mouths, juice trickling down chins, as what appears to be a line of votaries with saucer-shaped containers on their heads rises to meet us. Only Yannis the fig-picker makes this unnerving arrival human, by running to the skirts of one of the vestal virgins and tugging hard. 'There is Dassia,' Marie says. And she strides along the half-made balustrade and directs a torrent of words in Greek, in a low voice. We all stand, like children, as Yannis and his mother are addressed, and some furtive chin-wiping takes place. Then Yannis, shoved forward, comes up the last few feet of the path and positions himself in front of Marie. All at once it seems hotter than it has been all day—though the olives and cypresses down in the lowest point of the valley have lengthening shadows now. '*Efaristo para poli.*' It's clear poor Yannis is being made to express gratitude for the sweet. Marie smiles and steps off the balustrade, her kindly good nature restored. And the women walk round us, white cloths tied to their heads, and unload their burdens on the floors of the skeletal rooms. Stefanos, the chief builder, appears from nowhere and directs them, then they descend again, to walk to the limestone quarry at the back of land we still cannot believe is ours to build and live on—olive trees, figs and all.

Stefanos has his hands full, for he has to work without water here at Rovinia. It has to come round by sea—and here, as we walk into the embryo of the sitting room where my father has just a few days back added a yard to the length (it turns out to make all the difference, the decision to make the room eleven yards long, not ten), we gaze across the expanse of stone at the caique as it putters towards our little bay. Cement must be mixed on the beach—and, again, carried up on the white head supports—though there is a suspicion that sometimes the well at the foot of the hill, an unsatisfying provider of salty water, is drawn from in the mixing: it's quicker and less of a trouble than waiting for the next shipment of fresh water to come by sea. If this is the case, the house will be irremediably damp: no amount of the olive wood fires of which we dream will warm its chilly soul and we will be like maroons, living in a land that is cold and saline.

Today the beach is a hive of activity. Yorgos, the fisherman who shouts so loudly, even if he's standing next to you, that you look around for the Force 8 Beaufort gale, is dragging his small boat down into the sea with the help of a couple of youths from the village. It sticks on the logs, old timbers black with tar, and Yorgos practically deafens his comrades with his comments on the situation. The cement mixer, ear-splitting as a two-foot-distant lorry, churns out reassuring quantities of cement mixed with the good water brought by caique. The women—we are beginning to know Thekli and Dassia and Sula—go back and forth, an unending frieze of figures in clothes dusty-white with cement and limestone. And Stefanos, short and stout, with an air of cunning that his glasses and bustling manner fail to disguise, is up here at the site and down at the beach again with bewildering speed.

Today is not a day for the architect to visit Rovinia, that's now clear. But none of us regrets coming over in the car from Paleocastritsa, parking in the *plateia* in Liapades and walking self-consciously down the rocky street until it peters out and becomes the *monopati* down to the sea. Why are we embarrassed to go down this way? It's the presence of the men who sit in what is clearly their club that makes us want to avert our eyes, for we are recipients of a hail of questions each time we go by. '*Possa chronia?*'—How old are you? Are you married? and a good many others, including a whole exam to be taken on the subject of the Second World War; '*Germanos?*'—Are you German?; and, with a touch of yearning in the voice, '*Americana?*'

We may be some or none of these, but we know what we are not, when we stand idle and the women toil up and down from grove and shore to build the house at Rovinia. We are not capable of being loaders and carriers, their efforts show us that; but then, so it seems, neither are the men.

The sitting room, at eleven yards long and six wide, will be where we eat as well as where we sit, and there is talk of having a sofa made that is L-shaped, forming a room-within-a-room in front of and at right angles to the fire-place. A chair of the same design as the sofa will be made to fit in next to the fire—which will burn on a stone base, with the mantel high above. For eating outdoors, there's the verandah; and to go there we need a table long enough to accommodate nine or ten people. Already a mental note has been made of those vital clips, in use in all the tavernas, which anchor down the plastic tablecloths against the gloriously named winds: the Bora, the Tramontana, the Maestro and the Scirocco, to name but a few. On top of the plastic will go a simple linen cloth, equally secured. The prospect of resembling an outdoor restaurant is appealing to the pale-faced indoor-eaters we alas all are.

The question arises, where do we have made the long table—and, indeed, the sofa? What about the chests of drawers that will be needed upstairs in the bedrooms: three of these, one with double aspect to wooded hill and dazzling blue sea, and huge, where my parents will sleep; the other two at back and front respectively, one single and the other a double room with a view right up the valley at the back, designated for my still only eighteen-year-old younger sister Catherine. All must be furnished, simply and well—a lot to ask, or so we think. How can my mother acquire a dressing-table without having to disguise it with miles of unwanted fabric? How do we find simple things? Do they understand plain?

It turns out our suspicions were insulting to the Corfiot carpenters. Whether a long tradition of Venetian and then French design and excellence of handiwork had been the guiding influence on the island was impossible to tell; but a visit to the workshop of the wondrous Panayotis on the outskirts of the town showed it was possible to order solid chests in the best beech. A straightforward dressing-table, with the requisite row of drawers down both sides of the kneehole, would be no problem. Even fitted cupboards—for the small room that my father would use as a dressing-room when there wasn't a guest in need of it—could be manufactured in a short space of time. As for the sofa, the most ambitious of the Rovinia requirements, the small warehouse and carpenter's shop on the edge of the potholed roaring road leading into Corfu town gave an undertaking to construct and upholster one in a period of time that would have been seen as laughable at home. Prices, too, were much lower than we expected: after totting up figures on the back of an envelope on which he had sketched the articles of furniture required, my father's complexion took on a healthy hue. We decided to go on into town to celebrate finding this good place (Marie Aspioti, inevitably, had been the one to guide us to it), and only my mother's faint doubts—'We haven't seen what they're going to produce yet, remember'—prevented over-rejoicing. (However, Marie was proved right in her commendation: everything ordered that day was sensibly made and a pleasure to look at, the sole exception being the table for the bedroom overlooking the valley, which had a wooden-framed mirror on top, but refused access to anyone, tall or small, who sat on one of the rush-seated Van Gogh wooden chairs in front of it. Knees came up—and do to this day—bang against the underside of the table. The mirror, thus at a distance from the would-be user, looks blankly out into the plain, whitewashed room.)

This, however, was not to be foreseen on the triumphant day of the Corfu carpenters, and would not have mattered much if it had been. We sat in the taverna by the harbour at tables that were distinctly rickety—due to the cobbles—and ordered moussaka. The time of the year when the *melanzane*, aubergines, are at their juicy, deep plum-colour best is summer as it turns to the infinite early autumn enjoyed by Greece. It took some time to realise that Peter, our actor friend, wasn't ordering anything at all.

'What's the matter?' my sister asks. She is, as often before, quick to perceive the changes in mood of someone she likes—and she has psychic gifts too, as we've all noticed since she was twelve years old and obsessed with the Ouija board in the disused room in our house in Scotland, a room that ghosts would surely visit if they came at all.

'I've forgotten my point,' Peter says.

Both I and my sister know immediately what Peter means. It's hard enough being an actor—and Peter is still very young, only twenty-four—and he has had to endure a year's run in *Son of Oblomov* with Peter Sellers, the famous comedian taking the opportunity to mock and trip up poor Peter at every performance. No doubt he'd come out to Corfu to restore his equilibrium after this appalling experience. And what had we done for him? The house had taken over, causing friendships and perception to blur. The archetypal nature of the land at Rovinia—the olive grove, the sea—had made us insensitive to small human pains. 'What shall we do?' my sister asks tenderly.

Peter surprises us by saying he'd like to go and see Marie Aspioti. We hadn't even noticed that he'd been taken with her, though the scholarly detail that Marie supplies on all subjects to do with Greek drama, history and politics would be bound to enthral him. Her down-to-earth nature and brusque kindness would suit Peter's highly sensitive nature. 'We'll go after lunch,' my mother says, who is prone to ingest crises of this nature and quietly try to solve them.

When the *carpouzi*, the irresistible watermelon, has been

eaten (and Peter did have some of that) we decide to skip coffee and go in search of Marie. First we try her house, the Villa Rossa, an ugly nineteenth-century building put up by her family and still lived in by Marie and her mother, despite the fact that the family suffered financial ruin in the Second World War. The walled garden, for all the desuetude of the once-grand house, simmers in the afternoon heat, the orange and lemon trees, with their trunks white-painted against insect infestation, giving a formal air in contrast to the generally run-down atmosphere. Shutters, green and flaking paint peeling back to reveal the rotten wood underneath, hang from their nails by the windows. Is Marie asleep inside? It is of course, as we guiltily remember yet again, the siesta hour. 'I don't think that brother of hers will allow her a siesta,' my mother says sadly. She's told us of Marie's brother's insistence on hard work and low pay at Corfu Travel, the bureau the family has set up on the hill leading down to Capodistriou Street (the main thoroughfare) in the town. Marie would almost certainly not be permitted a snooze during the hot months, if there are tickets to be booked. And those booking tickets are as often as not foreigners, as oblivious as we sometimes tend to be to the two-to-five siesta rule in Corfu.

Marie's office is efficient and cool, with a fan riffling the papers and brochures on her desk. Posters for Greek island ferries (some I already know and dread for their discomfort and casual approach to safety) hang on the walls. Her office is a back room, and a pleasant young woman in the front room stands behind a tall bar of glistening dark wood. Her name, we learn, is Athina—and I find myself wondering, with so many reminders of the *Odyssey* on this island, why Nausicaa never seems to crop up as a girl's name. It can't be the obvious reason, its similarity as a word to nausea—for nausea isn't known to the Greeks, although they have plenty of words for being sick.

It's as I'm sleepily thinking these thoughts (the siesta has reached me, even if I'm not back in the Tourist Pavilion in Paleocastritsa, lying on my bed) that the door to the back room is flung open by Athina and we are asked to enter.

Peter goes straight to Marie and—as if she's known all along that he's in need of sympathy and understanding—she asks him about his next part. Or, when she sees this isn't decided yet, 'What would you really like to be in?' she asks in her quick, clipped English.

To our surprise, and possibly Peter's, he replies, '*The Merchant of Venice.*'

'Ah, the quality of mercy is not strained,' says Marie gently. 'It falleth as the gentle rain from heaven . . .'

Peter goes over, walks behind the desk and sits on it, his long legs dangling. And he starts reciting—reciting furiously and brilliantly—great chunks of *The Merchant of Venice*.

'Let's go and see if Olympic have new schedules for the autumn yet,' my mother suggests in a low voice. And we troop into the front room and stand by the long bar that is almost shoulder-height.

'So how do I help you?' says Athina, as the voice, muted now by the wall and closed door between us and Marie's office, recites on, Marie staying enraptured by the twice-her-size actor perched on the desk.

'Flights to London via Athens,' my mother says; though none of us listens to Athina's reply.

We leave the town, the arcades with their shops and cafés fast asleep in the afternoon sun, the cricket pitch—a relic of British occupation—scandalously dry and brown in the heat. The sea, so different from ours on the west coast that it could belong to another country, gives off its usual unappetising smell. Shall we drive home, stopping perhaps at the little church where the resident *papas* grows onions and herbs in the shade of the modest Byzantine dome?—or shall we head up to Gastouri, a village on the hill?

My friend Mark's cosmopolitan cousin lives at Gastouri; and it's a place, I know, which seduces those in search of the 'real Greece': for the Hellenophile, our seascape is too heavily surrounded by forest to be anything other than Italian (though in fact Rovinia and the coastline down to the south on the west side of the island must resemble archaic Greece, before goats nibbled all the vegetation away; the dusty brown landscapes so beloved of the traveller in Greece are relatively recent).

'He may be exploring the Epirus,' Mark says. 'But we can try.'

I can feel the temperature drop, as Mark's cousin Justin and his superior and eclectic knowledge of all things Greek come once more into the conversation. Justin will undoubtedly cause us to feel inferior when it comes to understanding Greece. Worse still, we actually have the temerity to plan to come and live here. 'We'll have to ask them over to

Rovinia,' my mother says in a low voice. We can all sense the failure of the meal we have come to enjoy at the humble Tourist Pavilion: *souvlaki* (lamb kebabs), chips—and fish if something's come in that day. Justin and Christina, who is as fiercely 'authentic' as her husband, will probably bring a picnic: olives, feta, bread. My father likes his bit of skewered lamb at lunch.

Gastouri is on an unmade road—the old olive trees for which Corfu is famous flanking houses that are like the houses in faded frescos, of stone that is the palest of washed reds, a blue that looks as if the colour has been sucked out of it into the sky, a yellow like melons when you cut them open and all the white pips spill out. An inland heat we never suffer on the windward side of the island has pre-served trees, houses and sudden shockingly green patches of watered and tended grass in a bell jar, a kaleidoscope where the shimmering caused by the excessive temperatures squeezes all together in patterns and stripes, pure and two-dimensional. It's impossible to tell where the shadow of a black wrought-iron gate or cypress tree ends and the real entrance to a house begins. My father, at the wheel of the rented Ford estate car, drives slowly over the bumpy stones in the road. Even so, he almost goes straight into the gatepost of the house where Justin, refuting the siesta in a way that is surprising for so international a traveller, is lean-ing from a ground-floor window. The watermelon walls and faded green shutters behind him give an air of a decrepit fruit-and-vegetable stall, with Justin, blond and wispy-bearded, tending the produce right through the heat of the day. 'I'm delighted to see you,' he calls out, recognising first his cousin and then us, whom he has briefly met in the town. 'Come through, come through.'

The inside of the old house that Justin and his wife take each year from the Corfiot owners is as much a tapestry of beautiful near-dereliction as the view of the old village from outside. Chairs stand—just about—with backs lopsided or cane seats missing altogether. A large round table, once polished but now bearing marks of ancient inks and paints, is laden with journals in sprigged-paper covers and pressed wild flowers, making an autumnal atmosphere in the heavily shuttered room. Dried grasses and faded poppies lie on yellowed paper. A sideboard holds Venetian glass, red and white goblets and a decanter containing something that looks suspiciously like black wine. 'I insist you try some of this,' says Justin. 'Ah, here is Christina. She will explain how this wine was made, she was a part of the process.' And he laughs, throwing back his head to reveal a long, scrawny neck only partly camouflaged by the yellow beard. Christina, dark and determined-looking, greets us all and goes over to the decanter. A tiny chink of sunlight penetrates the almost-dark room and dust motes dance on the Venetian goblets, ghostly fireflies lit by the ruby glass.

'I'm so looking forward to seeing the garden,' my mother says, saving us just in time from the satanic wine. 'I've heard so much about it.'

Even if this is an exaggeration, we know Gastouri's most alluring side lies precisely behind those houses that seem so impregnable, due to their gates and tall, funereal cypresses. And we also know that Justin and his wife have left the garden to run wild (the owners have apparently no interest in it). As my mother wishes for an almost wild garden at Rovinia, on the terraces that lead down to the grove, this has certainly intrigued her. We know there is a steep incline on the far side of the row of habitations, and that the road runs along a ridge, particularly narrow just here. 'This is the way we love to live in Greece,' Justin says, throwing open a french window into the garden, the shutters swinging as he impatiently pushes them back. 'You may desire to embark for Ithaca, from your Liapades Bay'—exchanging glances with Christina, as if they have already discussed and dismissed the insalubrious air at Rovinia, the climate that will not be congenial to gardening—'but we here may well have found Arcadia.'

We have to admit—equally with exchanged glances—that, for all his affectations, Justin is probably right. These old roses (I can sense my mother wondering if they could ever grow in the stiff salt breezes from the sea) that ramble along the stone walls look as if they've been here two hundred years since the Venetians built the house. A heavenly scent comes from them; and as we take our eyes from a dwelling-place that seems to have grown into a bower, we see beds of lavender and canna lilies that grow up to the windows from an unkempt border running along the wall. The garden here doesn't seem all that wild—until, gazing down the steep bank immediately below us, it's possible to see what Justin meant by Arcadia. He also meant, without a doubt, a Greece in miniature: a grove such as Pan would have played in; a sense of mountain, grotto and sacred place. Enchanted, we make our way down the bank.

A small piece of woodland on the hill at Gastouri

comprises the 'wild' area of Justin's carefully untended retreat. Pines give a delicious cool, and their needles make a fine, soft carpet. Cypresses add an air of dignity. Oleanders gleam in the undergrowth; pink and white blossoms in very dark green leaves form a garland on the head of the hill. Ivy grows up a column and then runs to a table, stone inset with a marble mosaic, rough and unpolished. An intense silence, broken by the sound that pines make when a breeze, not palpable at ground level, touches their branches, leads us all to fall silent in the middle of our words of praise. 'This is where we like to sit in the evening,' Justin says, and he leads us down through the pines to a clearing high above the mountains, the distant sea and the sun-baked houses of Gastouri. There is another table, wooden and by now so rickety and ivy-entwined that it has become a part of the forest. Wicker chairs are discernible in the deep shade of the trees.

'It's like being outside the monastery near Delphi,' Christina says, 'Ossios Loukas. Don't you agree?'

It is time to go home. We're given a rapid tour of the house—distempered rooms, old boards on the floors with spaces so wide between them that I see my father's eyes roll in disbelief. On the wall of one room the name of Christina's mother has been scrawled, in red paint: 'Maman Natasha'. Then back to the dark dining room, past the unsavoured black wine and out into the now-heavier gold of late afternoon.

'It *is* beautiful, after all,' my mother says as we drive on the unfrequented back road from Gastouri across the island to the west.

Everyone agrees. But I can't wait for our house to be built: the house that will be white and square, with the wide doors that my father always insists on, and the bright light from the sea.

I'm on the beach loading a bag with pebbles. They'll go down on the new paths and flights of steps to the house, which rises, a frame almost ready to be roofed, behind me on the hill. I know the patterns we'll lay them in: circular, concentric, like a mosaic already laid on the table left behind on the small terrace of the cottage—or minor *bastide*—my father bought in the South of France in the 1930s and then returned to, married to my mother, to restore when the war was over. I feel I know the shapes without even opening my eyes—we ate bread and honey from the Alpes-Maritimes on the surface of that pebbled table, with wonderful coffee to wash it down. But here, despite the repeated swirls and geo-metric order of the mosaic, the familiarity of the contrast between grey, white and rose-tinged, I can see a very different enterprise is foreseen. The *bastide* near Valbonne, unspoilt then, a pocket of lavender and olive trees as unlike those here as they would be if they belonged to another species, was vis-ited in spring and summer, for holidays. The rooms were old, low-ceilinged and dark—but no-one cared. Here, it will be real life, everyday life that the new house will provide. The stone platforms on the paths going down to the sea—and on a table in the sunken garden, once it's dug out—will be no more than reminders of those now-cancelled days. All the same, I feel a twinge of nostalgia as I search the shoreline for any new throw-ups from the sea. There had been yellow butterflies in France, and umbrella pines, which gave off a scent recognisable even after years away. Here, I've seen only one brimstone, attaching to the flowers of cistus and broom, and a red admiral or two. For all the assurances that there are swallowtails to be seen here, I've yet to come across one. Something about the inland nature of those small fields and blue lavender beds could never be found here, I sense: there's just too much salt in both water and air.

As if to underline the rightness of my thoughts about missing France, and the pleasures of driving through meadows bright with buttercups into Antibes, with the sputtering of Lambrettas along a wide boulevard leading to a café-fringed sea, a sound identical to those long-forgotten pop-poppings rises above the (today fairly buoyant) waves. I look up, Juan-les-Pins vanishing from my mind, and see one of the fishermen approach in his boat. There's nothing new about that—the bay appears to suck in and spew out small craft virtually every hour of the day. It's Yorgos—and it is he, as so often, who comes up to the shingle bank with a last roar of the exhausted engine and leaps out, up to mid-calf in the clear, warm water—but there is also another figure in the stern of the boat and it is he who commands attention. Despite announcements made daily on the lack of availability of a new pump for the well that Achilleos has dug just above the line where beach meets grass (or brown, baked earth, as is the case at this time of year), here is Stefanos the builder with something in his arms. It isn't a child—or a consignment of watermelons—or anything that could be

expected, at this stage in its erection, to go in the shell of
Rovinia House. It must be—and here I draw in my breath as,
Stefanos, with a casual gesture that would have been proved
fatal by a larger-than-usual wave, throws the heavy object,
apparently wrapped in a tarpaulin, on to the beach.

The shouting begins: it's the magnified shouting we've
all grown used to, whenever we come over to Rovinia. But
in this case there is news to be conveyed. Collas the architect appears on the nearly completed terrace and peers
down. I see Thekli, her skirts grey with building dust, join
him and shade her eyes as she peers down at the beach.
Then excitement starts to spread. The pump has come. The
powerful new pump, which will draw the fresh water
Achilleos has so effortlessly (as the architect predicted) discovered at Rovinia. Easy! All that is needed is a good
strong pump.

For some reason the commotion makes me apprehen-
sive, and I go on sorting pebbles as Yorgos and the two men
who invariably materialise out of nowhere heave the small
fishing caique up on the tramlines of ancient timbers. I run
the stones through my fingers—blue-grey, some of them;
never enough black; white as snow, nearly white, deep
cream. I wonder, as I put those ripe for the mosaic paths into
my bag, if these are pebbles washed down in Homer's time
by the river in full spate, before it made an estuary with
sandbanks six feet high, like a roofless tunnel leading to the
sea. And I think of the story again: the young woman, a
king's daughter, and the stranger made welcome in her
father's splendid palace three bays to the north. Why did
she never try to seduce this handsome man washed in like

the pebbles on to this shore? All other maidens, witches, sirens tried to keep Odysseus for themselves. Was it because this young woman wanted to observe and record, and not to marry and lose her voice to any man, that she turned away from her first idea of marriage? Had Nausicaa—as I knew had been claimed by certain scholars at the beginning of the last century—been the real writer of the *Odyssey*?

The shouting up beyond the high-water mark has grown in volume. My parents have joined Stefanos; and Achilleos, the valiant digger, has appeared. As I walk slowly up to become a part of the scene—fresh water! we must all have in our minds images of drinking deep in the excellent cold water of Rovinia, and the atmosphere is one of rejoicing—I see a couple walking along the grove and crossing the riverbed just below the well. I remember—these must be Thodoros and Maria Mazis, from Liapades, who will keep their house and land up in the village, but will also live in a house behind Rovinia House, just now going up. A site with olive trees all round it, and terraces going down into the deep valley—the part furthest inland at present a vegetable patch cultivated by the Mazis family, but soon to be the sheltered garden where roses and lilies, so my mother hopes, will grow. Thodoros's family were also the owners of the land where Collas has placed our four walls and our terrace. I wonder at first what he and his wife—who have applied to live here and work for my parents, he as boatman and care-taker, she as cook—must make of the familiar plots turned to such eccentric use. But it is possible to see, as I come up close and take a quick glance at their faces, that the selling of this bit of land, on bad soil and open to every rogue wind that chooses to blow in, has not been a painful decision for the couple. They look friendly and relaxed, their expressions that Greek mixture of transparency and humorous cynicism it would be impossible to find in Italy, directly across the Ionian Sea from where we stand.

Thodoros comes from an intensely religious family (his father a holy and respected man in Liapades, his mother responsible for all the farming work, and out all day on the family *stremata*) and is dark, with commanding good looks. He has a jaunty air and appears—quite a mistaken impression, as it turns out—to be something of a popinjay. Although the young couple already have an infant son, Spiro, they are completely dependent on Thodoros's father, and he and Maria must ask for money for everything as well as, in Maria's case, permission to go into town. Every *drachma* they earn here will be handed over to the patriarch.

Maria, whose family name is Repoulios, is one of six children—a jolly, singing family of which she is the eldest daughter. Brown-haired and bursting with vitality, it's possible to see her as the *belle* of Liapades, a lover of all the social occasions that the village can offer. She immediately shows herself as a leader of festivities: red handkerchief held high, she's known to head the dancers at weddings and fairs.

The look of amusement on both Maria's and Thodoros's faces, as I am soon to discover, is not so much due to the wild shouting and gesticulating of Yorgos—who has dragged up his boat, as he so often does, so they say, within one-eighth of an inch of the huge breakers forecast in tonight's storm, and has joined the celebratory crowd—as to the sight of a woman, in black as before but now with hair flying loose from her snood, who crosses the riverbed at a run, in hot pursuit of two furious billy-goats. '*Katzikaki, katzikako,*' the by now well-known cry rings out. And I see my mother and father, as the goats rush to the well and Anna Georgiadis dashes after them, turn and exchange glances with Thodoros and Maria. They all burst out laughing. Things are going to go happily here—despite the fact that Stefanos can't assemble the pump, and the first rumblings of thunder can be heard in a sky suddenly the colour of a bad bruising. Things will go well here at Rovinia. We're all going to get on.

Anna Georgiadis has a reputation for violence. My mother's mastery of demotic Greek, which is in its early stages at this point, can run to the understanding of stories about the village; mine, which I embarked on a couple of years before (travelling in the Peloponnese and northern Greece with a learned older friend, I suffered shame at my inability to return the hospitality offered everywhere with at least some information about myself—'How old are you? Is this man your husband? How old is he? *Saranda pende?*'—and eyes would roll, though Fred, my companion, was neither husband nor lover) has deteriorated badly.

I find I can understand, perversely, when a rush of words, accompanied by the steady gaze of the Greek raconteur, are directed at me. But the slow, careful enunciation of one who knows he must reach the limited comprehension of foreigners has me at a loss. At present, as we walk up the path, I'm at a disadvantage. The teller of the tale is up ahead of me, with my mother, who has asked about Anna Georgiadis, so

I cannot see him as he speaks. And—as if to mock the betrayal of his friend, a cock crows continually on the rocky way up to Liapades. I'm aware we could be hearing the truth about Anna—or a version that comes down in a bias of cousinages, doctored by reason of feud or loyalty.

'Anna Georgiadis's husband died,' says Yannis, whose brother is mayor of Liapades; Yannis himself is a fisherman.

'Ah, she is a widow,' my mother puts in.

'No, not at all,' Yannis says. 'She beat her husband, that is the fact about Anna Georgiadis.'

I conceal my surprise; and I note my mother does the same. The woman with the goats, who forced my father into paying more than he paid any of the others for the land, is not someone with whom it would be safe to be closely involved.

'And she beats her second husband also,' Yannis says. Even lagging behind on the path, I can hear the delight in his voice. Clearly, we do not know all there is to be known of the redoubtable Anna Georgiadis. 'She is a very smart woman,' Yannis continues, as the mad white dog tethered to the railing of the first outpost of Liapades life, a house on four pillars, the lower floor reserved for animals and fodder, comes into view. I try to remember the advice given by travellers in Greece to those who come across aggressive dogs— a frequent occurrence and potentially fatal. *Sit on a low wall*, runs the adage. *The dog won't attack you if you're sitting down.* Unbeknownst to family and friends, I have been trying this out; but the last time I lowered myself nervously on to a wall, the stones slipped and cascaded to the ground, causing a frenzy of rushing and barking.

'A smart woman?' I call up the hill to Yannis. I don't

want to lose the story of Anna Georgiadis—but the dog is now gobbling the end of the olive stick I carry with me for just this reason. 'What kind of smart?'

'She has much gold jewellery,' Yannis says, turning and looking straight down at me so that I can understand more easily. 'And this is why the new husband stays with her. But they wanted a child. So—' he shrugs, and shouts to the dog, which falls quiet. 'So she is too old and she cannot have a child—'

The rest of Yannis's words are lost in a cacophony of cocks' crows from the patch of land just under Liapades. It is the noisiest place in the world here, I think, wondering how the rural idyll of peace-and-whispering-sea can be realised with a village like this just up the hill. At night, as I know from expeditions by moonlight to swim and picnic in the place we will one day take for granted, dogs chase shadows down the grove. But Corfiot dogs—with the exception of the crazy white canine on the path—are too likeable to blame for nocturnal barking. Brown—generally—with white patches, and with the air of Labrador and collie combined, they have intelligent, enquiring faces. Only too often, as we've seen driving on the island, they're run over by the maniacal lorries indigenous to Greece. I promise myself, if we have a dog here, that it will be locked up at night.

Yannis has finished his tale, which appears to include adoption and cruelty. We pant on, over great scissor-shaped rocks, which stick up from the mud and shingle that make up the Liapades roads; and as we go I note, as I do every time, the totally primitive quality of the villagers' lives.

They have neither running water nor electricity. Water is carried up by the women on their heads or in the saddlebags of donkeys, from a well at the foot of the steep Liapades hill. Light is provided by oil lamps—and often there is none at all, so the place is plunged into a medieval blackness once night falls. Lavatories are open holes in the ground. Cold and rain all winter bring chest complaints, pleurisy, pneumonia. It occurs to me that childbearing must also be unchanged since earliest times, and I find myself directing at Yannis, as we walk past the closed and paint-peeling wooden doors that open into the yards of the houses, the type of questions so often asked of us, the *xenoi*. 'How old is Anna Georgiadis?' I call to him. '*Ti?*' Yannis swivels round and looks at me with the blank, shut-off expression I've seen in Greeks when a question is unanswerable, or the time has passed to prolong conversation.

'*Dhen pirazei.*' At least I know the demotic for the end-lessly repeated mantra of Greece. 'Never mind.' I see I was tactless; besides, for all I know, the husband-beater Anna may be here, behind one of these doors. But the fact is that it's impossible to tell from her appearance just how old Anna Georgiadis—or indeed any of the women here—may be. Work and climate make crones of women considered young still in western Europe or America. A *ya-ya*—granny—can be in her thirties. Plenty of women known as *pro-ya-ya*—great-grandmother—have reached the mid-century, no more. Possibly Anna Georgiadis, despairing of bearing a child for her handsome young husband, wasn't old, but simply unable to conceive.

We arrive at last at the end of the lane. Not one of the

houses we pass reveals its life to us—the high whitewashed walls and bolted door set in the plaster and stone give a Moorish feel. This must be an Arab influence, one thinks at first. But Corfu looks to the west, and not to the east: the Turks invaded, but were never able to colonise here—and, despite the super-sweet Turkish coffee, the *loukoumi* and the lilting Eastern music that plays day and night on the radio, the island bears the memories of Venetian and French ownership rather than of Constantinople.

The lane comes to the corner where the men sit—White's Club, as my father calls it. They're in the *cafeneon*, which has one side facing the *plateia*, the central square with the church and high steps built into its far side, so that grocery shops sit perched above the rest, in this village that goes up and up.

Here is our car. For sweets and toiletries we'll go to Stavros, the only supermarket, which stands on the crossroads, six miles down the road into town. But we'll buy what we can here—notebooks in blue shiny covers, ouzo for drinking in the evening in our rooms at the Tourist Pavilion. We'll be shopping here one day soon, for the house. Everything will have to come down the path on donkey or mule. Will it really be viable, this new way of life just now being hammered and knocked into existence? 'Everything is possible,' my father says. Then we go right into the darkest and deepest recesses of 'White's' taverna, to ask if there's any mail. Addressed to Rovinia—a new address for a new life.

The new electric pump for the well, admired for its power, turned out to be too powerful after all.

Sweet water, to be tasted like every drop in Greece with a knowledgeable smacking of the lips (a glass of water accompanies everything that's put on the table, even the simplest *meze*), had confidently been expected from the deep well dug by Achilleos at Rovinia. Even with the use of the old pump, we had expressed delight and relief at the fresh water so miraculously drawn up from ground as hard as the baked clay for the pots and pitchers you see in a village courtyard: a desert-red, suitable for storing water but not for yielding it.

We're standing round the well when the new pump goes into action: but in truth there is so much going on by now that the producing of water is overlooked by us as being of prime importance. The roof tiles of Rovinia are on, and it's this historic occasion that the Greeks celebrate with a great feast—which is precisely what we are about to do. The tiles arrived—by sea in the caique, like everything else—and we stand on the beach admiring these slabs of fired earth, the covering for our future house: faded, and ranging from deep ochre to a colour that's like the sun when it goes down over the Monkey's Head. It's impossible not to reflect on the lives, deaths, disappointments and joys that these roofs of old and abandoned houses have overseen. (The battle, at first, had been with Stefanos, whose determination to provide new tiles, glistening, uniform and a bright orange, 'treated' not to fade, had been prolonged. There was disbelief—and then, as was the way with Stefanos, a sudden rush of understanding, 'Nai, nai'—as he visualised the derelict buildings from which the tiles would be removed, and the ensuing profit.)

For our feast, there are long wooden trestle tables being

carried from the caique on to the beach and then into the grove. Luckily, the weather is calm. The Feast of the Assumption, 15th August, the day on which the entire Mediterranean drops tools, moves to visit families, celebrates and prays, has passed; as has, particular to Corfu, the Feast Day of St Spiridon, four days before. The intense heat, said to subside after the Virgin's ascent to the heavens, has indeed gone down since a spectacular storm that had us wondering, over in the well-protected Tourist Pavilion at Paleocastritsa, how the new house at Rovinia would handle the lightning. (But we have been assured by Collas that a lightning conductor has been ordered for the new roof.)

Along with the tables, which we set up, along with Thekli and Dassia and the fourteen-year-old Athina, are upwards of forty chairs. Wicker demijohns of retsina are lugged up the grove by Yorgos and Yannis. Knives and forks, borrowed from Paleocastritsa, go down next to the white paper plates, these brought down the path from Liapades in the saddlebag of a mule. A smell of cooking meat begins to make itself noticed as far down as the flat bottom of the valley. Four sheep are turning on a spit, up the hill behind the newly roofed house. No wonder the well is only visited from time to time. Someone says it's bad timing—as well as bad luck—that the new pump needed electrical repairs before it can be primed to bring up fresh water; a pity it all had to happen today. General agreement—but we don't know yet just what bad luck it will turn out to be.

For now, nothing can go wrong. The sun shines, the sea has taken on its coat of many colours: deep royal blue, turquoise, soft pale green by the cave where the sun never reaches, where it is, as I think it, Kubla Khan's sunless sea. The olive trees are dancing in the slight breeze, turning from young girls decked in bright-green ribbons to tossing grey heads, and back again. My son is here—it's the school holidays—and he stands looking in pleasure at the little boat he will be able to row across the sea in, to Yefira, the neighbouring bay, or Alipa. He is seven years old, eight in November. He has named the bright-yellow rowing-boat 'Swift Swan'.

We walk up the forking paths where the women go with their loads of bricks and cement, and when we reach the half-made terrace we turn away from the path and head towards the sharp peninsula that juts out into the sea. Known as 'The Point', this is one of my son's favourite places; and the layers of the dark rock-face there are black and shining. In order to go down it, we must go in single file, through flora that turns marine as we walk: sea pinks, tall white squills, which push like stumps out of the inhospitable ground but then flower as profusely as asphodel, sea vetch yellow with an intricate, pretty leaf.

Before we go right out to the point—and sometimes it's possible to forget this is part of Rovinia too, this long inky snout pushing out into deep water—we stand on the path a while. Here it refuses to go to the point, choosing to turn on itself like the tail of a snake and return to the village, or plunge down through bramble and scrub to the beach. We look back at the house, a frame with a skeletal wooden roof on which the tiles and guttering have been placed. My son remarks of the bricks that they're 'not like our bricks'—and it's true, they are hollow and oblong in shape. But I see the

women, as they rise slowly with their head pads, as caryatids: even if they do neither brick-laying nor plastering,
the weight of the house is borne by them. 'Come on,' I
say—and the child walks first, down over the scissor-sharp
rocks to the stone bench, carved by Nature to seat a king—
Poseidon perhaps—so that he can sit all day long on a
throne and overlook the sea.

Shouting down below brings us from the daydream that
sitting on the point invariably brings. It's to do with the
sheer hugeness of the blue Ionian that rolls out from here,
with the porcupine's nose that is the point shelving away
steeply on either side. And the vertiginous cliffs at Yefira,
visible from here as they are not from anywhere else on the
property. Cliffs tall and madder red, with cypresses and
olives growing down the sides of a deep ravine, plunge to
the sea. We say we'll row over to Yefira—there's a tiny taverna there, reachable only by boat or down a difficult path,
the one the fishermen take when they leave their boats
there in tricky weather. We'll go there, and sit right on the
edge of the sandy beach and order egg and chips, and then
we'll row back again. And Coke, of course; even in a place
as inaccessible as this, where there's a fridge, there's a Coke.

The shouting brings us back up the point, on to the path
and down the scramble to the beach. We see the tables
under the grove are filling up: the landscape spews out
guests for the great day of celebration in Greece for any new
house owner: the day of putting on the roof. All those concerned with the building of Rovinia are here, and a good
proportion of the village it seems; and the roasted sheep are
being carried down. Wine is poured and bread goes round,

brown and gnarled as the roots of the olives that guard the tables in the grove. There is laughter, and a kind of anarchic gaiety—and as my son comes near, he's seized by one of the women and then tossed from arm to arm.

But there's another kind of shouting to be heard, from the well at the foot of the path where the first steps will go up to the house. I see Stefanos, a gobbet of mutton hanging from his lips, leave the table and leap the dried-out riverbed to arrive at the site of the beautiful new pump. Heads turn to watch him as he goes.

Somehow, it's impossible not to know the outcome of Stefanos's brief journey—though it feels as if he has crossed continents and swum seas by the time he comes back.

The men at the well had turned the pump to full blast. And what came up, from the depths, was not the fresh water we had tasted at first, drawn gently from a shallow level. It was brackish. It was salt. It was the sea.

The lunch winds on, becomes an afternoon, a day, a cycle of the Greek sun. Retsina flows in glasses lent by the *xenodoxeion* in Paleocastritsa, and the frieze of figures around the long tables jerks into life, like early cinema. Yorgos the fisherman is dancing, silly-faced with love at the young woman who twirls at the end of his reach; two caryatids, brown-cheeked and no longer with faces whitened by limestone from the quarry in the trees behind our table, are coming up the beach from the clear, pale sea. Singing—songs that are strangely sad and haunting when all around is gaiety and celebration—echoes down the grove as it may have done thousands of years ago, when the women from Alcinous's palace disported themselves on the banks of the river here.

A grandmother—a *ya-ya* (or a *pro-ya-ya*), she is too heavily shrouded in black clothes to be anything other than an emblem of extreme old age—appears at the head of the grove, where the formality of the two lines of trees dissolves to disused terraces, dappled with shade beckoning for the after-lunch siesta. She tethers her donkey to a tree and is called to, told to join us and eat. The *xoriatiki* salad, of feta, carrots and tomatoes, with its punctuation of dark olives and tiny strips of lettuce and cucumber, is carried in a bowl down the length of the brown earth-hard floor of the grove where we sit. Then the mutton: Yannis shouts out a joke we can't understand, as a long bone glistening with fat and hanging with gobbets of meat is broken off and also carried down to this figure of ancient Greek drama. Does she curse us, or bring us good fortune, on this all-important day? Who is she and where is she from? But for the moment her appearance, after an initial chill, is causing too much merriment for anyone to tell us what we want to know. We'll hope instead, as the stranger at our banquet eats, that the giving of hospitality, though unexpected, has brought us luck.

The sheep, still turning on the spit as the day wears on, have not been hung—and, drastically, have not been cooked with herbs—and I find the taste, well, too sheep-like. It's the way the country people here like it, evidently; but as the greatest scent of Greece, the mix of rosemary and thyme, sage and camomile and honey-giving broom wafts down to us in the summer heat, it does seem odd that these are not stuffed into the mutton grilling over the fire. One of the best medicines known—the *tsai tou vounou*, mountain tea, which cures headaches, malaise, stomach pains and anything you care to name—is concocted from the magic wild plants on the heights of Pantokrator, or the range of towering hills above the Plain of Ropa, which stretches out beyond 'our' village of Liapades. Are the herbs, then, seen as prophylactics or medicines, rather than culinary delights? I can't stop myself wondering what the reaction would have been if I had secretly stuffed the glorious herbs supplied by Nature into our singeing sheep.

People are sleeping on the terraces now, under the olives, and they look as if they are lying on bunks made up for the purpose; soft, green beds (for there is grass higher up, above the burnt floor of the grove: the comfort is sublime). Someone in our party finds the first clump of cyclamen, down amongst the stones and pebbles in the deep cavity where the torrent, as we've been told, will rush down so fast in winter it will take our breath away. At first I think, mournfully, of our approaching departure: the cyclamen must be a sign of autumn; my son returns to school and I to work, in London. The party will most definitely be over, for at least another eight or nine months. But then, as I hold the small, mauve flower in my hand (the dark, distinguished leaves come later: it's too early for them yet), I understand that it's impossible to tell, in Corfu, when one season succeeds another. There is a perpetual spring; and Marie Aspioti tells us, as the little posy of cyclamen goes into a wine glass of water on the trestle table, that she has seen narcissi out already, on a country road on the way up to Strinilas.

'Where the turtles live, under a hump-backed bridge,' she says. 'And a big colony of snowdrops—they usually come in October, along with autumn crocus; the stem, as you know, is the same colour as the bloom.'

Marie has confessed to a love for England that consists mainly of a passion for robins—her favourite book, in a life-time of serious English reading, is *Lark Rise to Candleford*. It's obvious why snowdrops thrill her—but then it is odd and exotic, somehow, for spring and winter and summer and autumn to be so mixed up together, as they are here. The thought of a climate without frost, however hard it may rain on this sometimes Tuscany-resembling island, is difficult to believe.

The house, its cement frame ready for pipes to be laid and electricity to be prepared (but God—or indeed the *Deii*, the gods, as the electricians are named—alone will know when this may be), stands above the resting builders, carousing fishermen and gossiping women in the grove and olive terraces below. Will it ever be ready for habitation? Since my mother and my younger sister, on their way home from a business trip with my father to Australia in January 1965, saw the cement frame of Rovinia, another eight months have passed. It's tempting to see the roofed building as readier to move into than, of course, it is. Will the pebbles we've brought, and laid in Roman patterns in cement, make good platforms along the path, where wild olives will seed themselves and geraniums will flower from the blasted rock?

Above all—and I know my father thinks gravely of this, as he conducts a conversation in mime with Yorgos (they seem to understand each other well; even to be highly satisfied with each other's incomprehensible answers)—above all, my father thinks of the plumbing at Rovinia and of the expensive, all-important Panyatockis Report. Will the fat file of questions and answers supplied by the Athens plumbing engineers Panyatockis come up with the impossible, in Greece: modern plumbing? We have all visited hotels and houses, tavernas and bars, some exclusive in their nature, others humble, but all with one thing in common—the lavatory and accompanying waste basket, in which used lavatory paper has to be placed. It has been firmly decided that, even if Rovinia House is to set a precedent, this is what we shall try for: a bathroom or WC that contains a lavatory and not a waste basket alongside. The Report has promised four-inch soil pipes, and other sophisticated improvements. But we all wonder if the very nature of Greek plumbing, along with the ubiquitous 'Niagara', the loo with snapping chain and thunderous cistern, won't triumph over us in the end.

Now the feast is over. Clutching the bouquet of cyclamens, we return across the bay to Paleocastritsa, shamingly grateful for the calm sea and lack of necessity to do what the villagers are doing, which is toil up the path on the hill to Liapades. The summer seems to recede as a stiff breeze gets up halfway, and we arrive at the little crumbling jetty drenched to the skin. For all the perpetual spring that the flowers provide, a true sense of the coming autumn has descended. The Tourist Pavilion suddenly seems bare, the beds hard and the walls white and empty. It's time to go back to London, leaving a house that may, or may not, still be a wreck when we return.

II

The gentle half-mourning of the cyclamen and autumn crocus in Corfu seems like a dream of high summer, compared with the gales and rain that have set in at home.

It is autumn, 1965. My parents' empty house in London has begun to take on the look of a house that knows it's about to be abandoned: tables are cunningly askew, bulbs not replaced in lamps. Staying on in Corfu for the plastering at Rovinia, the soon-to-be exiles seem to have disappeared into the distance, as questions about the future begin to reassert themselves. While I let out my house (which has the advantage of one large room, and the disadvantage of possessing almost no other rooms at all), I take time off to consider the giant step they are taking. Will they really be happy to have to drive all the way to the chief village of the district, Skripero, to collect mail and, even, make a phone call? It's said that letters can be collected from time to time at 'White's Club' in Liapades—but the thought of important missives being swept aside by players of *tavli* and drinkers of endless *ouzaki* is chilling. On the other hand, why should there be any important missives in the first place? Hasn't my father now retired from the family firm— and even sold it, possibly in order to paint the sea and the cliffs and the villages with their steep streets and flocks of sheep, unmolested by mail? But I worry on. What if there is a telegram that needs to be delivered urgently? Again, the image of old men in cloth caps, the sun like a policeman enforcing coma through the long hours of the afternoon, brings little relief from anxiety. I can't help admiring my father and mother, all the same, for cutting themselves off from their previous life so entirely. I see them in my mind's eye as hostages to the sea, on the waterless land they have bought on the west coast of the island of Corfu. If it's flat and calm, they'll be able to go round to Yefira, or on to Alipa or Paleocastritsa by boat—and, more significantly, fresh water in drums, along with other supplies, can be brought to the bay and then carried up to the house. If it's stormy and rough, they are captives: there will be, as an Italian visitor remarked in astonishment on being taken upstairs at Rovinia, '*Niente, niente, niente*'. Maybe this is what's impelling my parents to shrug at the absence of amenities: a kind of Zen blown in on the wind of the Sixties has affected their way of seeing the world, along with the concept of necessities. This, however, would be greeted, if put forward as a theory, with laughter.

If there's no date given for electricity—and if, as we in London suspect, no date applied for, when it comes to a telephone—then at least the essential nature of water is recognised and catered for. Two large rainwater cisterns will be constructed at Rovinia, one behind the kitchen and the second just below the house that will be Thodoros and Maria's, on a terrace bordered like the rest with a long path of pebbles arranged in mosaic patterns. Enough rain falls in winter—so we are all assured—to fill the cisterns and enable us to drink and even wash sparingly. Those who remark on the prevalence of goitres amongst populations drinking only rainwater are politely ignored.

The failure of the well with its too-powerful pump has been a blow, no doubt about it. Digging must wait till spring now; and everyone knows somehow that Achilleos does not possess the magic gift of finding water. There's now talk of finding dowsers and diviners.

This is the season for olive picking and the women from the villages will be bent in two, gathering olives from amongst them. I begin to want to go out to Corfu again, urgently; but I know the shortcuts we are smiled and waved through in the summer months are no longer open to us now. Olives make a dark, viscous mush underfoot; and there's a sense of criminal trespass if one walks uninvited over the livelihood of the families of Liapades.

Besides, there would be nowhere to stay, should I take it into my head to enjoy the autumn, my favourite season, on the west coast of the island. The Tourist Pavilion in

Paleocastritsa—and with it the smaller Living Lobster—
have both closed for the winter. It would be *fin de saison*, if
there was ever really much of a season going, in what is still
a remote resort serviced only by a potholed road. I fantasise
about going to a village—Lakones perhaps, so high on the
mountain above the site of King Alcinous's palace that
black clouds envelop it half the time—or Gardelades, with
its pretty pink and rust-coloured houses. I'd be offered the
famous Greek hospitality: the spotless whitewashed room,
the lumpy bed with a scratchy quilt, the hollowed-out 'feet'
that are one step down from Niagara and waste basket, in
the outdoor toilet. But I'd be exploiting this hospitality,
with a house in the process of going up in Rovinia Bay—
and to try to be anonymous would be impossible. I go back
to my freelance work for a magazine, and wish myself in that
pure, blue air—while wishing at the same time for rain,
which will fill the new water cistern that is fondly believed
to have gone up at Rovinia, at the back of the house, over
the kitchen.

Some people, 'Cousin Justin' and his friends amongst
them, are holding out as long as they can against the actual-
ity of what is happening on Corfu (on the coasts, anyway).
And I recognise there's something of them in me, when I
state to friends that Corfu is still 'unspoilt', that nothing
very much has changed since the Durrells, in the days of
Prospero's Cell and *My Family and Other Animals*. In fact, the
airport is being enlarged at speed. Tourists walk along the
miniature rue de Rivoli constructed by the French and
overlooking the (so British) cricket pitch in the centre of
Corfu town. Buses rumble across the island, and with

terrifying daring, having gone through Paleocastritsa, mount the vertiginous hill to the monastery. Pottery quite unlike that used by Ulysses on his visit to the beautiful and reclusive daughter of the King is appearing on stalls and in jerry-built shops. Here and there, waving in the wind and smelling as strong as the spit-turned sheep at our own roofing feast, a huge white knitted jersey is suspended from a rope, a price in red ink attached on a label. *To saison* (the season) has begun to be spoken of, and naturally with delight and respect. Here, with the visits of these strange aliens, comes a recompense for the long years of hardship, war and starvation so familiar to the Greeks.

Films, obviously, have a lot to do with this surge of interest in Corfu—and in Greece generally. From every radio blares Theodorakis's 'Never On a Sunday'. Melina Mercouri, her eyes filling the amphitheatre around her, becomes the symbol of the nation. (Anthony Quinn, with *Zorba the Greek*, has brought sightseers in their—as yet—thousands.) And transistor radios, invading the groves where 'Cousin Justin' and his ilk pause to listen to the pipes of Pan, are now, in popular locations, producing a mix of *bazouki* and pop, with wailing Turkish-sounding songs thrown in.

In London, still suffering the separation from Greece, I read the poems of Cavafy and Seferis and count myself fortunate if I can find editions with the Greek on one page and the translation opposite. I go and see Cacoyannis's film *Electra*—which doesn't mean I miss out on Melina Mercouri and Anthony Quinn: it's just that Cacoyannis's masterpiece has me on the edge of my seat. The murder of Aegisthus, lover of Clytemnestra, by her son—and the strange but oddly successful epithet placed in his mouth at the stabbing, by the translator Patrick Leigh Fermor: 'You . . . fop!'— enthrals me every time. As for Irene Papas, I feel I've seen her in the flesh, so powerful is her performance. The great Rachel must have been like this—or Sarah Bernhardt.

I'm dreaming of all this one day in the spring when calling round to my parents' house in London. Replacing the double snowdrops in small brown ceramic pots are grape hyacinth, dwarf iris and white paper narcissus. 'We're going out to Rovinia, whether it's ready or not,' comes the message from my parents a few days later on the telephone. 'It may be rather cold, but there's plenty of firewood. And paraffin lamps—let's hope they work better than the last time we tried to get it right.'

There are no direct flights to Corfu. Getting there means flying to Athens, waiting in the café with its roll-top counters displaying *baklava* and tired fried eggs, and then some five hours later boarding the local flight to Corfu.

My parents camped there a few months back, before returning to London—but for me this, the spring of 1966, is the first time I shall sleep at Rovinia. The house has taken two years to build—we don't know yet what is still lacking in this brave venture—and all we want to do is to feel properly, happily, at home.

Inevitably, we arrive in the dark. Rain falls, quietly but persistently. Thodoros meets us and we drive through the night to Liapades. From the village, we walk down the invisible path, holding torches. Somehow or other, after hearing the great breaths of the sea on the rocks below us in the blackness, we know we have arrived.

❧

'The torrent is down,' my father shouts from the terrace. These are the words that wake me, in the single bed in the guest bedroom (one of a pair, made of hard wood that catches the leg as you round the corner to climb in; but last night we were all too tired to notice. The mattresses, as hard as the wood, occupy more attention).

It has rained and rained. We lean from the bedroom window, still half-asleep—it's two hours earlier in England and the torrent has caught us with jetlag. Brand-new shutters, not yet painted, creak as we push them open. We came down the path in rain, and stumbled miserably about while paraffin lamps were lit, their plumes of black smoke going happily up into the whitewashed ceilings. We expect rain, and more rain—like in Scotland, where it's a furnishing that comes with the valley, the silver birches and the wastes of bracken: a curtain of fine rain.

But here, the sun always wins. In recompense for the long winter, the suitably named *ximona*, with its echo of moan and shriek, the sun has returned to the land where it belongs. The sea, blue and innocent of the recent storms and gales—these betrayed by the high-water mark, a scribble of black seaweed and dark stones—lies as blue and flat as a plastic sheet. Small boats have already appeared, like bugs on the surface of the now-placid expanse: some are fishing boats and others, larger and further out, appear to be carrying loads from the south of the island up to the north. It's so clear you can almost fancy you see Italy.

But the torrent takes precedence over everything. On a

Calor gas stove down in the (unfurnished) kitchen, Maria fries eggs and pieces of cut-up bacon. The sun dries the leaves on the wild fig trees below the kitchen door, by the entrance to the long store room under the house, the *stoa*. Orange trees serve as another reminder of the power of the Greek sun, and the very different climate we have entered here; their fruit is thick-skinned and open-pored, like an eighteenth-century courtesan's complexion, and there is an underfelt carpet of pith to be cut through before tasting. Lemons hang as bright as light bulbs down by the cypress trees at the head of the grove. Wild rosemary attracts butterflies, the first I've seen here in quantity: the tiny blue, not unlike the pale sapphire rosemary flower that draws them; a yellow brimstone, the colour of an old-fashioned duster; a black-and-white butterfly in a complex pattern (and what this is I don't yet know).

The landscape is as untouched by drama as today's brochure-blue Mediterranean Sea. Here is a place to build a house with impunity, we think, going out on the newly built terrace and then round to the apron of stone in front of the drawing room, which will be a garden for flowers in pots, and for growing climbers against the dynamited rock-face. Nothing dangerous or alarming can take place here, in this bay with the grove of olive trees that runs right down the middle of it, to the sea.

The torrent removes such placid thoughts at first glimpse. For one thing, how could such a volume of water come rushing down without any prior warning? What would it be like, to find oneself caught in mid-spate while crossing a riverbed usually so obstinately dry—rain or no rain? How fast does it run, this thunderous cataract? A river without the staying power of a river, it dashes past and then disappears for another year.

We all stand on the banks of this thrilling, unexpected arrival in our midst. It could be an animal or some monstrous early amphibian, scooting down over land before rejoining its natural element, the ocean. There's something archaic about the torrent, dragging down its necklaces of beer bottles and village rubbish from on high. It is frightening, in the way the Gorgon in the small museum in Corfu town (a Medusa dug up within the past few decades in a field on the island) terrifies and warns: there's more to fear than simply wishing it away, the untameable water proclaims. You can be drowned, annihilated—or turned to stone, before being carried out to sea.

This is just what has happened to the great brown river itself, as we note with astonishment. Maria, the frying of eggs long forgotten, is running down from the terrace of the house with some of the wild energy of the torrent. She is pointing and shouting—but we can't hear her against the roar of the water, and we probably wouldn't understand anyway. There's a general peering in the direction of her gesticulating arms—and it's impossible not to imagine a black-sailed ship spotted on the horizon, a harbinger of terrible news, which in our ignorance as foreigners to these ancient shores we are unable to comprehend.

What Maria is showing us is the extraordinary—and instant—new landscape created by the torrent as it reaches the beach and goes out into the sea.

We run in an estuary with inlets of water brown from the hills and then translucent, where it mixes with seawater from the bay. Dunes, created from sand most certainly not there just a short time back, make pale, pristine swellings above the shingle of the beach. But the beach is no longer as we remember it. Most of the pebbles have been swept away. Boulders like lurking monsters are visible in a new, deep shelving where the land ends and Ionian Sea begins.

The torrent makes a great fan of dark water as it hits the soft blue of the sea. Tea-coloured waves rock the little fishing caique that Yorgos tries to bring in. A miniature disaster, in Rovinia Bay, seems certain to take place.

The sea accepts the alien rushing water from the woods and hills. For a time, as we stand with Maria, bare-footed on the miracle sand, we cannot believe the huge, spreading stain will ever go. Like an oil slick, it winds sinuously around the small boat; there is much shouting; the appearing of other fishermen as suddenly and inexplicably as the descent of the river itself; the craft tugged into the just-formed estuary and then up on timbers still red and blue from last year's painting.

Silence. We hardly dare turn to look upstream—for, as we had suspected but had been incapable of visualising, there is no 'upstream' now, only the stones and pebbles of the riverbed, already drying in the sun. The torrent has worn itself out and has emptied itself into the sea.

For a few hours, however, I knew I saw the river Nausicaa came to with her maids. It would not have been going at such a speed—this I had to allow—but its presence in the middle of the slender valley, with the wild olive-clad hills on either side, changed the landscape Homer had (perhaps, who knows?) written about, back to its original dimensions.

☙

It's time to look around, now that the drama is over. I try out walking the length of the sitting room, several times, and am pleased with the sense of both economy and space: the small ash-wood table at the far end, looking out on the apron of flat stone and the beginning of a collection of plants in pots (a morning glory, embracing a rose, makes a trumpet of blue against a backdrop of the now-muddied sea), is just big enough to seat six, in a carefully contrived separate area from the rest of the room. The large custom-made sofa, an L-shaped Great Bed of Ware, will take at least nine people—the number that can sleep at Rovinia comfortably, now that the Wing, or small guest house along the path, is pretty well ready for habitation. And the rug, woven in the town to a design made by my mother, doubles the sense of expansiveness in the long, vaulted room. Brown and white, muted and geometric in pattern, it lies on the tiles from Grasse and makes just the right contrast with the pale rose of unpolished baked earth. My father's study, with a rug this time of a strong weave of blues and white, can be shut off entirely from the main room, but may also become a part of it when the very wide door is left open: here, on a trio of shelves above those built to house the hundreds of files he has brought out from England, stand the china deer, a stag and two does, that I remember liking as a child, when they stood elegantly in a glass-fronted cabinet in our home in Scotland. Now, pale in the strong Greek sunlight, the delicate faces of the deer appear strained and anxious. They are about as far, I think, as I cast my mind back to early Cretan ceramics and sculpture, as one can get from the culture we have now entered and hope to make ourselves a part of.

My father seems at first as removed as the ornaments he has carefully brought to Corfu with him, from the shapes, colour and atmosphere of a Greek island. Not in the sense that he is delicate, like the deer: there is no fragility in this man in his late sixties who sits on the balustrade on the terrace, now that the spectacle of the torrent is over, and mends a model aeroplane for my son. Nor is there a trace of anxiety, in this foreigner who does not know the language and, I suspect (as it turns out, rightly), has no intention of learning to speak Greek in the country of his adoption. My mother, who works daily at her vocabulary and grammar, will look after that—but it's impossible not to wonder what would happen if anything were to befall her. Without a telephone, there would be no hope of contacting anyone in England . . . but these thoughts, as I realise, are pointless. My father would, somehow or other, get on very well. He may err on the extravagant side (didn't he meet an old man amongst the olives on the way up to Liapades the last time he and my mother were out here; and, on being asked in a forceful manner to supply a radio, the next day drove into the town, bought a transistor radio and handed it to the old man in the groves?)—but, even stranded here on his own (an unlikely prospect) there would be little chance of disaster.

The files in their dusty covers on the shelves in his study make it finally possible to understand the desire to leave England and return there only on the most exiguous of visits. Born as the second son in a family peppered with eccentrics, whose extravagances would have shown my father's modest purchase of the gift of a radio as not even worthy of mention, my father was to become a symbolic father of the whole tribe on the death of his elder brother in the First World War. Each file (I would never open these Ali Baba jars, the contents a record of the dispersal of treasure rather than a glittering pile of accumulated riches) bore the name of a brother, cousin or distant kinsman or -woman, and inside were their demands for assistance, both financial and emotional. Out of a sense of duty, from which this survivor of the Battle of Gallipoli (aged fifteen) and the Second World War never deviated, the files accompanied him even as far as Corfu. Letters were answered punctiliously. But the mere fact of a distance of a thousand miles between Rovinia and London—before coming out here the house in Scotland was made over to my elder half-brother, and more burdens eased—must have been, whether admitted or not, a major reason for the move.

Upstairs, I am struck (not for the first time) by the extreme neatness of both my parents' rooms. Were they too indulgent with their children, in not insisting on a tidying of possessions and clothes? Probably; but to see the nautical precision with which my father has arranged his things in the small dressing-room at the end of the passage is to be reminded of the huge difference in his upbringing and ours. Banished to naval college at Dartmouth at the age of twelve, he learnt to brush his teeth to a strict formula, while not a second of the day could be wasted, and not an inch of space overlaid with unnecessary items. And in turn, looking in at this shrine to order, with the ivory-backed hairbrushes side by side on top of the chest of drawers built to his own specifications to house shirts and underclothes (a fitted cupboard contains the suits he no longer needs to wear, in the blessed freedom of Corfu, as well as the simple green tweed jacket and grey trousers for cooler days), it is his past as a sailor that begins to explain the decision to come out here to live. Of course! Looking at the albums stacked in the newly built fitted cupboard, I saw little but the sea there: in coming here, my father has revisited his nautical youth.

It's not surprising that Virginia Woolf heard the swallows conversing in Greek. Classical Greek, naturally—so I wouldn't understand much of it anyway; but listening to the swallows here, there's an intensity in the exchanges, the sharp, quick calls and succeeding staccato of rumination or response that do suggest a long-hidden language. Maybe the Mycenaeans could make it out . . . like Linear B, it needs a scholar to interpret the meaning.

The swallows are building nests at a great rate, in the wooden eaves under our verandah. They've come up from Africa—as the rain did, in the final coming of spring, red from Sahara dust and settling in long, pink swathes on the white-distempered walls of the house. The birds swoop, indigo and purple in the year's new sun, down to the valley floor for mud and grubs. Then, flattening themselves against their homes as they build, they make the semi-circular pebble, earth and spittle nests to which we hope they'll come back, year after year. The chatter and drawl become deafening, as they build. White swallow droppings are everywhere—on the blue-and-white chequered lino of the long table, protected from sun and wind by the verandah roof. Friends, Denis and Pauline, come over for lunch and tell of the almost total takeover by the swallows of their home near Skripero. It's a barn, and the birds have chosen the old beams, at their most tempting just above the bed. Sleep has become a matter of seizing a few hours before the chorus begins at dawn. But there's no two ways about it: swallows are the souls of dead friends, returning from an unimaginably long journey. They're the only birds who like to settle in human habitations. And they can no more be shooed away than a member of the family.

The house improves by fits and starts. Already in place are the upstairs floors of Swedish pine, a greyish silver, with thick wooden planks underfoot and no need for any but the simplest rugs, brought over from Metsovo on the mainland: ancient designs, red, a deep rose-pink and black.

The furniture for the bedrooms is in place, and in the room with the two single beds there is a Goldilocks sense of being the wrong size when trying to fit knees under dressing-table. I decide instead to use the folding serving table that sits, shrouded in red-and-white checked cloth, just outside the room; and thus the typewriter can be reached without spinal injury. The dressing-table has its own uses, however; and it is here that the mirror stands, also made by the carpenters in Corfu town. My face looks back at me, misted from the strange glass fitted in the oval wooden frame, and also askew, so that features are elongated and shoulders mountainous, like a fairground reflection. The chest of drawers by the side of the bed is, however, a triumph: drawers slide in and out, with none of the antique-pine shudder of such pieces back at home. Deep enough to contain clothing for all seasons, it has the pleasant look of one chest on top of another: old-fashioned but practical. And a door in the corner of the room near the stairs gives hanging space in a cupboard so large one can walk in and turn around. There's even a window in the cupboard, which looks down the flight of wooden steps, each stair garnished by Spanish tiles alternately a deep marine blue and white. Through the window in the cupboard the voices of Yorgos, as he comes into the kitchen below with a catch of fish, or of village children brought down by relatives of Thodoros and Maria to visit their toddler, Spiro, rise in ghostly fashion amongst the dresses and skirts and jeans hanging there.

The large double bedroom with its bare pine floor and high white ceiling is dominated by the sea. Three windows show the Ionian, and in the case of the window furthest from the door, the virgin Mediterranean jungle on the hill opposite, like the compositions of artists who put a frame around nature before sitting down to paint it. The sea is so blue it could have been made from lapis lazuli, beloved of icon makers. It's a blue such as was scratched by superstitious peasants from the eyes of painted saints, or worshipped as the robe of the Virgin, against a gold background of the sun. In contrast to the sea, which lies flat up against the window panes—or so it appears, and I begin to understand the skill of my father and Collas the architect, in siting the house and calculating the height needed, to give this illusion—the wood and hill across the valley seem humble, a green knotted wool tapestry such as a child might sew. The topmost boughs of the olives provide a silver thread, along the middle of the view; then, flat and perspectiveless, the tall scrub and dark cypresses, like pencils on the hilltop, reach up to the just-visible blue sky.

When it's stormy, the room becomes dramatic, suffused with a science-fiction light. Thunderstorms are hardly bearable in here, the lightning a violent signature across a darkening sky. We've watched a tornado in the form of a water-spout from these windows, as it spiralled elegantly out at sea: no-one dared express the hope that it would come in no nearer than the Monkey's Head, and the flashing beacon of the lighthouse there. Could we be picked up, in this house that was carried as stone and brick from quarry and beach, and returned to the water dashing up against the rocks below? Or would it take the trees like Japanese toy parasols and send them sailing up into its spray? We didn't know; and came downstairs to stand a little nearer to the ground, looking out from under the swallows' nests at the great column of advancing spume. The tornado went out of sight; and we waited, later, for reports of cars tossed over cliffs and uprooted trees. There was no news; like the torrent in our valley, like much in Greece, the drama was intense and then forgotten—until it came again.

The house from outside has a homely, straightforward appearance. 'Cousin Justin' and his wife, who do have to be asked over (didn't we go to Gastouri and see 'the real thing' there, the Greek experience as lived by a family of international expatriates: now it's time for them to pronounce judgement on our house without a history or a past), come to Paleocastritsa and we meet them in our brand-new caique.

The *Falaina* (little whale) is small and dependable, the size of the fishing-boats around here but with a wooden superstructure that it's possible both to sit on, in good weather, and cower under if the waves are coming right into the boat. The engine, deftly managed by my father and Thodoros, has a powerful, healthy sound to it, unlike some of the 'taxi-boats' now coming over increasingly to our bay with a catch of German, English and Italian tourists. Spankingly painted in blue and white, the *Falaina* is the apple of my parents' eye. 'Can this be us?' they ask, setting off for Yalli or Iliodorus, the unspoilt bays and beaches south of Rovinia, where the water is, if possible, even clearer and bluer than our own. A long morning is spent swimming from shores unvisited by any but the monogamous pair of large and clumsily formed gulls that patrol this section of the coast. We eat late, on those occasions, and sleep through the afternoon, like everyone else. But today 'Cousin Justin' and his wife are coming, and to meet them the *Falaina* takes us not away from civilisation, down to the south, but over to the bay already famous from Edward Lear and Lawrence Durrell, the bay that will undeniably be pronounced 'spoilt' by the cosmopolites.

Yet our visitors when they arrive are silent on the subject of Paleocastritsa. We walk down the jetty and board the small caique. We head out to sea—and turn—always an exciting moment, for it is then that Rovinia becomes visible from the sea for the first time.

The house, white and simple, sits on its hillside as if it was meant to be there from the beginning. The shutters are blue, just painted, but succeed in looking as if they have always been blue. The landscape all around, where the rock was dynamited, does look bare, there's no doubt about that. But already the scrub is pushing out its branches, the gorse is in bloom, and cistus, pink and starry-white, has burst into flower down by the stoa, which is guarded by a dark-grey cobbled wall that runs the length of the building.

'Cousin Justin' and his wife, who sit in the stern of the *Falaina*, publicly exchange glances, then rise to their feet and lean on the wooden roof of the half-cabin, to peer out at the fast-approaching Rovinia House. 'It's very like the Lubbocks", 'Cousin Justin' says. His wife nods agreement. We continue, glad for the silence enforced by the roar of the *Falaina*'s engine.

We none of us have any idea what or who 'the Lubbocks' can be. But the absence of compliments from our guests on arrival at our lovely house does lead us, later, to ponder— and then laugh—at ideas of what, and where, these Lub-bocks can have planned and built.

What we didn't tell 'Cousin Justin' is that at present we have no water at all.

The rainwater cisterns, promised for the back of the house above the kitchen and for the terrace under Maria and Thodoros's house (when they're down here, and not at home in their big house up in Liapades), have simply not been built. What water there is from the well dug last sum-mer is all right for washing down floors, or for taking (not very refreshing) showers, but it cannot be cooked with, nor can it be used on the garden. In the now decreasingly frequent rainfall, my mother rushes out to set pans and buckets on the terrace. For the first time in our lives we scan the skies for the welcoming sign of a rain cloud.

This oversight apart—and Stefanos vows the cisterns really are next on the agenda and will soon be installed—everything else in that line is here and (as it were) raring to go. The septic tank, of stone and cement, at the bottom of the long flight of steps that leads from the terrace down to the beach is in place. The bathroom facing the main bedroom and the shower room opposite the guest bedroom are elegant with their deep-green Tinos marble on the floor. A bath in the large bathroom, basins and an optimistic shower in the shower room—all cry out for fresh water. There's even a basin in the small room at the end of the passage, the room my father uses when there isn't a child or single guest in need of somewhere to sleep. He shaves after bringing up a jug of hot water—that is, if the buckets and pans outdoors yield any of the precious commodity. The rain water has had to be heated up on the Calor gas two-ring cooker, as there is still no sign of electricity.

All that aside, we agree the house looks stunning, both inside and out. The hall and kitchen—at ten square yards the same size as the long room where we sit and, if spring hasn't quite turned to summer yet, also eat by the windows looking out on to the growing garden of plants in pots—has a capacious cloakroom off it, and a WC. Both the square enamel sink and the loo are served by the brackish water in Achilleos's old well. The Panyatockis Report, still sitting prominently on the desk in the small study off the drawing room, has proved a good investment, even if it has cost a fortune. There are no waste baskets next to the lavatories at Rovinia. On the other hand, there is also no proper water supply.

The most beautiful part of the house must be the long room, and this beauty came about by accident. The ceiling is vaulted—which is of course always beautiful in a long, high room; but it was the addition of the extra yard to the room's length that caused the vaulting to descend in swallowtails to the corners. This rectangular room now looks as if it represents the flight of criss-crossing birds.

The flooring of both long room and hall is down, and exactly suits the austerity and grace of the walls. Ordered from France, the tiles are lozenges, not polished but matt, pale tongues of baked earth. The fireplace, tall and white, is tiled inside, and takes hefty olive branches for our evening fire. My father's pictures—he has set up as a painter, in this brave new life—begin to appear on the walls along with some of the oils and watercolours brought from London. A Venetian chest, a battered and faded sea-green with eighteenth-century white panels, stands at the near end of the room, by the door into the hall. Here the games for children, the backgammon boards and Scrabble, and the bottles for grownups sit in a musty gloom. Someone has given a sketch of Corfu by Edward Lear as a gift, and it stands on the mantelpiece. Everywhere else bears reminders of the sea: fossilised fish several feet in length, shells and pebbles from our own beach down below.

In August the first guests come, friends of my younger sister Catherine. They're perfect, as visitors to a house without either water or light: Mark (who my sister will marry

eight years later) is the first of the gypsy caravan dwellers, a
horse breeder from the West of England; and Millie comes
with him, a novice hippy at the very beginning of this
strange new movement. They are welcomed to Rovinia,
where to arrive is to have walked down through the groves
and perhaps to have become lost—as happened to one visitor from England at the outset of my parents' life there: the
wretched man, seized by terror, could indeed believe he had
been misled by the mischievous, luring dance of the great
god Pan. Soothing talks and several glasses of the fiery eau-
de-vie called *sipourro* were needed to calm him down.

No visit to Rovinia is allowed to go by without a trip to
the Plain of Ropa. Next week we'll go to Doukades, and
walk up the hill to the chapel of St Simeon. Later, we'll take
the car up to the village of Troumpetta, from which both
sides of the island can be seen, and where to continue is to
look right into the mountains-of-the-moon landscape of
Albania. We'll leave the car there and walk along the
rough, cobbled drove road along the side of the hill above
Lakones. From Lakones we'll walk down the operatic grove
of Athene to Paleocastritsa. Whoever volunteers to stay
with the car brings it back home—or as near to home as we
can get. But for today, we'll go to the Plain of Ropa.

The plain lies behind the village of Liapades and
stretches as far as the eye can see in all directions: an
ancient wild-flower meadowland intersected by brooks and
dilapidated barns, it's ringed by the huge mountains that
never seem to lose their colour, whether it's morning or
nearly night, a dark purple suffused in an even deeper blue;
and so, with the alternation of shadow and light from plain

to mountain, one feels constantly in the presence of good and evil simultaneously. We walk, collecting bunches of the flowers that grow there in such profusion: marigolds a bright orange that shines up from short, sheep-nibbled grass; lithospermum a treacherous blue denoting the presence of bog beneath the roots; jonquil and bee-orchid and clover in every shape and form. The sun, softer and paler on the plain than at home by the violently blue sea, warms us pleasantly as we cross crumbling bridges over half-buried streams choked with a weed that looks like water lilies. But the comparative weakness of the sun is a delusion. By the time we're back on the unmade road where we've left our car, the only vehicle for miles, both it and we are boiling.

The solution is to drive a few miles, leave the car by the side of the road—a bigger road this time, the main route to Corfu town and civilisation—and then plunge into the shadier part of the plain, where olive trees so old they're like the arms and splayed legs of petrified dinosaurs will give us a kindly protection. How quiet it is here! We go up the farm track, turn into a wilderness of long grasses and reeds, and find ourselves walking alongside a lake, a great pond fringed with bulrushes. Here the quiet abruptly stops. What is this sound like a disgruntled orchestra? What is all the croaking and wheezing, and where does it come from, but the black water itself, the pond with a million frogs.

As if to counteract the surprise, we make our own inter-ruption by bursting out laughing—not that this disturbs or interrupts the mating toads and frogs on the lily pads and under the muddy banks of the pond. We're in an auditorium of lust, a spring ritual not witnessed by a living soul—for it's clear this land is uncultivated; only the olives tended, their fruit picked at the end of the year. The frogs enjoy an absolute privacy.

As we trudge back along a track now sunnier—and hotter—than before, we hear the story of the more sombre aspect of the Plain of Ropa, a story that has come to my mother from the village. Once we have arrived at the car and begun the drive to Liapades, she points out a dark olive wood. On that north-facing slope, we are told, amongst that forest of dark trees, stands a terrible house. The house was lived in by an elderly widower, with many relatives in the villages around the plain.

One day, the widower fell in love with a nun at the local convent. She came to live with him, in his house on the Plain of Ropa. They were happy, and the widower decided to marry the nun.

One night, when the moon was giving no light in the dark olive wood, the men of the family—husbands of the widower's two sisters—came up to the house. They went in and killed the widower and the nun.

They had to do it, the relatives of the widower's first wife said. If the nun had borne children, where would their inheritance have gone?

The tale makes us walk in silence down the rocky path from Liapades to Rovinia Bay. Even the first astounding shaft of blue, which is the sea seen from the highest level of the path, fails to lift our spirits. Someone asks if the murderers were brought to justice. No, they had extraordinary good luck, my mother has been told. The crime took place at the end of the war and the amnesty meant that they didn't go to trial.

However, she adds as we finally arrive at the last turn of the path as it winds down to the house, they died soon after apparently, of dreadful diseases.

So many tales of magic and superstition come down the hill from the village that it's almost a relief to see the local *papas*, bearded and black-robed, appear on the terrace and then go to the kitchen door to hold a muffled conversation with Maria and Thodoros. Evil spells, cast by disaffected relatives, have injured people in Liapades, turning sister against sister, daughter against father and mother. There have been descriptions of the heavy weight of ill-wishing, like an iron mass deposited on the stomach; there are stories of trousers found with mysterious holes, and other inexplicable phenomena. The *papas* has come to bless the house. I can't help wondering if he's taking the holy water from our brackish supply, or whether he has brought his own from the *ecclesia* (which, in turn, must be supplied by the well at the bottom of the hill where the village perches, as immured in witchcraft as it was in the Dark Ages). For all my cynical jokes, I'm pleased the priest has come though: after all, I'm growing superstitious too.

My mother, more Greek already than any of us, has grown accustomed to thanking St Spiridon for lucky escapes and small 'miracles': like everyone else on the island she doesn't blame him if things go wrong. But on the whole we have come to agree that the introduction into the household of the small statue of the saint is a good thing. He stands on a table in the sitting room, at the end of the Live-In sofa, next to the fossils and under a Surrealist picture of a shepherd in a dream landscape. When the spiny stonefish are dusted, he sometimes gets turned inadvertently to face the wall. My mother can be seen righting St Spiridon, to ensure he is ready if a sudden need for him arises.

The *papas* walks with his leisurely tread from room to room, sprinkling as he goes. I pretend to bump into him, to see how seriously he takes this ritual of cleansing a house of evil spirits; and the answer is: very seriously indeed. Although facial expressions are hard to gauge in holy men of the Greek Orthodox faith—the beard, like a rampant attack of lichen, appears to take over entirely—there is no doubt that our *papas* is intent on his mission. He has even picked a sprig of rosemary from one of the bushes growing wild at the side of the steps. He waves it portentously as he goes.

As it turns out, there is soon something to thank the *papas* for at Rovinia. 'You may have laughed,' my mother says some months later on the phone to London, when she tells us of the house's narrow avoidance of total immolation. 'When the boiler was blessed, everyone laughed. But now, look what has happened.'

The tale is a dreadful one, and just what people are warned against, who choose to live in remote places where a visit from an engineer or plumber is greeted with an incredulity and joy accorded in ancient times to a god or his emissary. 'It turned out that the regulator for the boiler had been put in wrong,' my mother says, her voice, admirably enough, fairly restrained and low-key. 'None of us could tell this, of course. But the boiler caught fire. Out at the back there, it would have set fire to the whole house within minutes . . .'

Thodoros it was who had thought to go and check

the boiler, despite the warm farewells recently paid to the plumbers, the thanks and repeated cups of coffee. Something—St Spiridon maybe—had 'told' Thodoros (so it was later claimed) to go down the narrow passage to the boiler room at the back. Flames rushed out to greet him. Just in time, Rovinia was saved from destruction. 'Perhaps we should all have our boilers blessed,' was all I could say when the shock subsided. But the thought of looking in the Yellow Pages for a visiting bearded man with portable holy-water stoop and sprig of nursery-garden rosemary proved in the end off-putting.

Colonel Merrilees is sitting at the table on the verandah with the map of the Rovinia *stremata* spread out in front of him. We're a year on, into the fateful year of 1967, when colonels of a very different kind will take over Greece, but for now Merrilees is the sole colonel on our horizon.

Our new visitor from England, a tall, thinnish, stooping man with an ineffectual air and a small white moustache, is retired from life as a professional soldier. An army engineer, he found water in India—and, introduced to us through friends of friends, he will surely find water for us at Rovinia.

We gaze upwards apprehensively as Colonel Merrilees runs his pencil across the map. It's only too likely that a swallow—they're in full swing at present, swooping, squabbling, falling into long passages of slang and recrimination as they rush to feed young birds stuffed into the tiny nests—will whiten and obliterate the precious drawing of the boundaries and main points of importance of the land.

Already there have been meaningful splashes on the limestone floor, these being difficult to remove and generally, despite jokes about 'Cousin Justin's' reaction if he and his houseproud German wife were to see them, left to fade into the surroundings. A male bird, brilliantly navy-blue and purple as the sun catches its back and long tail feathers, has already flown right past the Colonel's head. Some of these anxieties make it hard to concentrate on what we are being told about the prospects here for water.

'We will dig here first.' Merrilees prods the map hard with the pencil tip. 'Shall we go down there? Let's go.' And he rises with military precision, narrowly missing a cascade from the eaves above. Our faces try desperately not to break into grins. 'Excuse me.' It turns out that the Colonel has brought a carrier bag with him, it's out on the terrace, and from this he pulls two hazel rods and an assortment of plastic knitting needles. Armed with these instruments of his magical trade, he sets off briskly down the steps at the back of the house, beyond the kitchen. The usual small crowd is assembled there, some sipping coffee and others a dark liquid from an unlabelled bottle, which is the new vintage made from grapes grown high above Liapades. Maria and Thodoros's guests stare in amusement at the elderly, respectable figure of the Colonel, and at the English who have bought this place and now believe they can wave a pair of knitting needles at the ground and summon water up from it.

It certainly does look eccentric, I have to agree, and the laughter is unrestrained as we follow the dowsing soldier to the grove. But what alternative is there? Achilleos's efforts have all been doomed to failure, even if the pump is set at a more gentle rate than at the time of the first disaster. Merrilees may well provide the water so badly needed—though I have an unpleasant sense that hilarity might lead the hazel rods to indicate an unsuccessful site, out of pure vengefulness. Something makes me wish, all the same, that the knitting needles hadn't been included in the kit. Just as Merrilees's boasts, made the previous day, of locating gold in the most unlikely places, are also best kept from the sceptical villagers, I feel there is a strong need to play down our own credulity and folly in inviting—and paying—this strange old man to come and prove to us that there will never be any water.

Of course, it has been a delight to many in Liapades to pass on, via our helpers here, that they'd always known Rovinia to be totally lacking in any possibility of finding the elusive source, non-salty and drinkable. They'd known all along. So our slipping into magic is only a confirmation of the impossibility. I have to remind myself, as we go down the last step through crumbling terraces now thick with irises and wild garlic to the spot decided on by Colonel Merrilees, that people here believe in beings just as weird and improbable as this stooping old man. How about believing that the patron saint, St Spiridon, came to Corcyra (as some would call the island still) in the saddlebag of a donkey, all the way from Cyprus? He was dead, of course; but St Theodora, also demised, and packed in the other saddlebag, is reputed to have held conversations with the holy corpse, who then went on to become the most important figure in Corfu. No-one does anything here without consulting St

Spiridon. No hairpin-bend accident spot lacks a shrine to the saint. *Pasca*, the famous Greek Easter, has him out in the streets of Corfu town, borne aloft in triumph. If people believe in St Spiridon, I think crossly as we stand, feeling rather *de trop*, round Colonel Merrilees at the head of the grove, then we can believe in the power of the hazel rod and the knitting needle.

Once the Colonel gets going, however, it's hard not to burst out laughing like the crowd now peering down from the top of the steps. The hazel rods, merely twitching at first, are now leading him into an extraordinary dance. 'Isn't it a bit . . . well, quick?' someone in our group murmurs. But by the time the words are spoken, Yorgos and Yannis, both just out of their fishing caiques on this auspicious day, have smelt magic and entertainment and are racing up the grove. The party by the kitchen door abandons its coffee and wine (but not cigarettes, never cigarettes) and comes jumping down the steps to see the shaman perform.

This was the Colonel's first well.

There were seven wells dug altogether in those early years at Rovinia. The pattern repeated itself: however careful the pump, however glorious the first draught of clear, fresh water, it was always by the end of the day brackish and unusable. (At least it stopped drawing crowds, this regular disappointment: there was sympathy for the old man who had clearly believed he could work miracles, and then could be seen to have been no wiser or better than anyone else.)

Before the end of Colonel Merrilees's stay, a further 'proof' of his powers was granted us.

We were all waiting for my younger sister Catherine to arrive from England. It was a stormy day; and Corfu airport, never considered the most technologically well equipped of Greek airports, was just about the last place any of us would have wished her to be at that moment. We had no telephone, and the long sprint up the hill to Liapades in driving rain and under thunderous skies would not have yielded, very probably, the arrival information we desired. The one telephone in 'White's Club' was frequently out of order; besides, we could tell, or thought we could, that the plane was still in the air. This was the worst possible situation, in one of the island's famous storms. Without proper equipment or air-traffic control, it was difficult in the extreme for pilots to judge a landing. Often the planes circled, or swooped down and then failed to land, only to roar up again, going on to Athens when fuel threatened to run dry. All of us were thinking of these contingencies as Colonel Merrilees spread a map of Corfu out on his knee. The pencil was once more produced; and with it he began to trace the road that runs due west across the island, branching off to Liapades before going on to end at Paleocastritsa Bay.

We're all on the white sofa in the living room, the sofa that's like a room with three sides, and so we can see, as Merrilees's doddery hand follows the urgent signallings of the pencil on the map, the turn-off that leads up to Liapades. 'She's here, Catherine is here,' pronounces the dowser, and he makes a triumphant pencil cross on the map. And, arriving twenty minutes later, drenched to the skin, she was.

The seventh well was good. It had taken two visits from Colonel Merrilees over a period of close on two years and a variety of surreal discoveries—from the fish and eels found in the first well, eighteen feet deep, on the day of the glorious feast of the roof, to the passage tall enough for a man to walk along, which Thodoros found leading from the base of the sinister first well, to an unknown inland destination. Smugglers? Pirates? The underground walkway, closed by rubble, will never yield its secret. We still talk of the fifth well, where Achilleos found a big rock. Colonel Merrilees advocated dynamite—and, despite efforts to improve matters by lining the well with bricks and cement after the ill-judged explosion, the water never was sweet.

So it's a wonder to begin to feel clean, washing and taking showers in water that is only very slightly brackish; no comparison with the hidden seas brought forth by the previous six attempts. Colonel Merrilees, staying on to oversee the fruits of his genius, beams when we pass him on his perilous perch on the verandah. He holds up a map of Britain and declares, 'There's an awful lot of oil in Middlesbrough!'

We still drink and cook—and water the garden—with rainwater from the cistern, forgetting quickly the days when God and a few pots provided our entire supply. And the sunken garden that my mother and Thodoros have made is grateful for the newly available rainwater, the rest of the household needs having been taken care of. A large stone oil-jar from an olive press in the village, long ago out of use, is Thodoros's gift to the garden. It is older than his grandfather, more than a hundred years old, so Thodoros tells us; and he tells us also of the time there were thirty oil-mills in Liapades, the olives crushed between two huge stone wheels dragged round, until as recently as 1960, by horses. Petrol-driven machines came after—then and now, with the advent of electricity to the village, the mills are electrically operated. For all the new, efficient modern methods, Thodoros stands over the Rovinia olives when they go in the mill—in case we get fobbed off with someone else's duff crop when no-one is looking. The residual mush from the crushing was—but is less so now—turned into bricks for burning.

The stone jar—they could store up to two hundred gallons of oil or water—looks monolithic, important, in the centre of the rectangular, lowered patch of ground, bisected by paths with brick borders and visited warily by bluetits and boldly by crowds of house sparrows. Already there is a sacred-site atmosphere here, thanks to the plain, uninscribed stone; and it's impossible not to wonder at the source of religious terror and belief: did the priestesses at Dodona, the oak grove on the mainland, who worshipped Zeus with nothing more than the wind and the groves of those magical trees, demand guidance from a slab like this one? Of course, the olive tree is god on this island, and the old stone jar held the oil of countless numbers of olives before that particular press fell into disrepair. On Corfu, where almost five centuries ago the Venetians paid in gold for the trees to be planted, the olive, which remains unpruned, grows much larger than it does anywhere else, and yields fruit from October until June; far longer than, say, the olive trees of the world-famous Kalamata—where the trees are heavily pruned and all fruit stripped off in two or three weeks.

The garden is, I decide, the most romantic you could possibly find in the Mediterranean. Something about its being hidden: it isn't merely low, beneath the last terrace in the crumbling staircase of grey stone, but shielded on all sides, so that, on entering it, both life above and the sea at the end of the grove become no more than memories. Cypresses stand guard by the low wall, with an opening over a soft bed of pine needles to the garden that is beginning now to look like a painting, or a tapestry. On the 'house side' is a jacaranda tree, which will grow rapidly and burst each summer into blue flower. At the back a small grove of lemon trees has gone in, and at the far side, where a wooden bridge has been built to cross the riverbed—high-banked and forbidding here, dark under the olives and with sharp stones no-one would wish to clamber across—nature has supplied Rovinia with a magnificent Judas tree, blood-purple all spring from the blossoms named after Judas Iscariot, the Corfiot betrayer of Jesus. So the 'sunken' garden is like a room, and at the curved stone bench under the lemon trees at its furthermost end there is not, even on the roughest day, so much as a whisper of the sea. A room quiet as a library in its grove of trees; with only a sudden splash of bright blue at the end of the grove, visible between the boughs of the cypresses.

Here, my mother has planted paulonia, with its mauve/blue flowers, and the red rose 'Madame Isaac Pereire'. Aquilegia (columbine) is blue also—but otherwise the garden is white: syringa, and white roses that climb right up the low wall on to the terrace beyond; white freesias; jasmine and bushes of large white marguerites. In spring, wild flowers make another picture, just outside the confines of the little garden: the dazzling white star-of-Bethlehem, and the pink/mauve anemones that are named after the Greek wind. Two terraces above the garden, a glade of agapanthus, a different blue again, as soft and yet commanding as a hyacinth, stand under the vine trellis just set up there. 'We'll have lunch here on Easter Day,' we say; and we come down, Colonel Merrilees and all, and build a fire near the opening, in the stone wall, to the magic garden. But even the Colonel's special powers can't get a good blaze going— he is, after all, the spirit of water, not of fire—and we have to wait a long time before the grill balanced on olive twigs gives us anything edible.

Today we're following Maria from her house behind Rovinia, up the path to the village, to the betrothal party for Dassia, a Liapades girl who has asked us—with typical Greek hospitality— to come and celebrate her engagement to Nicos, a boy we've met only once or twice.

Maria, who knows everything and everyone—and is, also, related to half of the village—has told us bloodcurdling stories about girls and what happens to them if they throw away their virginity. So I'm surprised to learn that an affianced young woman moves into the house of her future husband as soon as the engagement party is over, and lives with him and his parents for at least a year, maybe longer, until they can afford to marry. One girl, Angeliki, had been the subject of scandal and reported cruelty, the first year we came out here: when she was found making love with a man, her father picked her up and forcibly carried her home, where he sat her down on a brazier of burning coals. I don't care to bring this up, with Maria striding ahead over the rocky path to Liapades, so I ask instead, in the modest demotic I have managed to learn, what the customs are and what we should expect, at Dassia's engagement party.

'We will go to the house of Dassia's parents,' Maria shouts back down to me. 'You will see, Nicos has bought Dassia a new dress. But he is not at the house—for this, we will have to wait.'

Dassia's parents' house turns out to be halfway up the (staggeringly steep) village main street. Motorbikes come put-putting down from the *plateia* as if there was no likelihood of meeting women of great age, bent double on donkeys that are themselves bowed down by the huge bunches of firewood tied to their sides. Then there are vans—the Greek lorry with its megaphone shouts: *Papoutsia* (shoes), *Sindonia* (sheets), *Pezeta* (towels)—that bounce off the walls of houses medieval in their fortified, blank façades. Do the motorcyclists not know about cars, I wonder desperately, as an ancient estate wagon (it turns out to be ours, with my father at the wheel) crawls up a street no more than two yards wide? People duck into the grocery shops, and peer out from the gloom under an assortment of plastic piping, ancient smoked sausages like petrified eels and rusting machinery. When another car, freewheeling cheerfully down from the square above, rounds the hairpin bend halfway up the street, I close my eyes and follow Maria into Dassia's family's house, grateful but guilty at my lack of desire to be there to help with the results of the ensuing crash.

However, there comes no sound of colliding metal; and I don't have a chance to meet Dassia's parents, because I'm almost knocked down by an army of young girls who are making their way, heads piled high with blankets, clothes and bed linen, from the courtyard to the door out into the street. 'They take everything for Dassia,' Maria turns and tells me, as the girls, some so dark they seem Turkish, others blonde and blue-eyed, push past and out of the *avli* (the yard filled with lemon and orange trees, concealed behind the high walls of Liapades houses). 'Now'—and Maria in turn pushes me to a flight of wooden stairs leading to the first-floor living quarters. 'We are just in time now to see Nicos when he is brought here.'

Dassia comes forward to greet us. Maria is clearly seen as a leading 'character' in the village—as indeed she is—and the fact that she and her husband are now employed down at Rovinia brings shy glances followed by a warm welcome. I ask her mother, who laughs and talks with Maria as the procession of girls makes its way out into the street, where they are setting off to, with their strange cargo.

'To Nicos's house,' Maria says, translating for the mother. 'All this is for Dassia—very beautiful things.'

It is hard to imagine what the main street of Liapades must be like by now; and I decide not to try. The sight of the Rovinia party, all generously invited, appearing in the door-way of the courtyard, just as the last bearer leaves, almost reduces me to hysterics. Yet, I reflect, there must have been somewhere to park—even if the word 'Parking' seems totally out of place here. And the motorcyclists and the old women on donkeys—and the even older man who made up his mind to bring out a rickety chair from the grocer's shop and sit in the street on it—and the van selling household goods and clothes must all have found somewhere to put themselves, so that the procession of girls with Dassia's trousseau on their heads can walk in full view of the inhabitants of Liapades, up to Nicos's parents' house. It's a miracle, indeed.

We're here, waiting. One last component of the village congestion must fall into place. Once the girls have gone, moving Dassia's material possessions upwards, the fiancé must himself be brought in.

But I—and I think the whole Rovinia party too—am overcome with surprise at the entry of Nicos to Dassia's parents' house. Like a football star, a sporting hero or victorious soldier, Nicos comes carried aloft in the arms of seven or eight young men.

Now it is Dassia's turn to disappear. As Nicos, laughing, is run to and embraced by all the children who are his future in-laws, an expectant silence descends on the company. A van, doubtless stuck on the road beyond the courtyard walls, hoots loudly. Then, amongst us with the same speed and insouciance as Nicos had shown in his improbable entry, Dassia can at last be seen. She wears a dress of embroidered silk of a deep rose-pink, given her by her fiancé.

The party begins to warm up. Little glasses of kumquat liqueur are handed round, as tooth-stirringly sweet as the cakes and pastries that follow. Nicos and Dassia stand together and someone takes a photograph. And we all laugh as the van outside gives one last blare of the horn and rumbles away.

Delicious smells are wafting from the kitchen at Rovinia, and we're drawn in to see the table almost covered by a huge baking tray with slices of *melanzane* (eggplant or aubergine) awaiting the next stage of one of Maria's magnificent moussakas. There are several dishes in preparation at once: chicken *xoriatiki* (as made in the village), which I've tried again and again at home but without ever achieving the taste of this apparently simple chicken-baked-with-herbs-and-potatoes concoction of Maria's; *keftedes*, the thyme-and-sage-packed meatballs, to be eaten with a tomato sauce freshly squeezed from the red fruit, and sprinkled with the short-leafed basil that we now grow in pots on the balustrade of the terrace outside the kitchen door.

My mother and Maria exchange recipes, and Maria, who is a natural cook, takes as readily to exotic suggestions like Floating Islands—sweet yellow custard dotted with blobs of fluffy white meringue—as she does to lentil soup or stew. Today we're embarking on a courgette soufflé. I own that my preference is for *kolokithaki* (courgette) as it is mostly eaten in Greece: boiled, cut into long yellowish-green strips and eaten tepid with olive oil and lemon juice. Something in the vegetable, as odd and idiosyncratic as, say, globe artichoke when eaten with an accompaniment of a glass of plain water, comes out when (frying and baking avoided) it is simply immersed in boiling water for five minutes, the oil and lemon imparting a flavour straight from Heaven. But the soufflé is delicious, of course, and Maria enjoys our efforts with it, pleased when it rises and philosophical when a stodgy base remains just that.

Maria is telling us about Dassia's musical gifts, as we stand in the appetising fug of the kitchen. It's agreeable to reflect that it takes only an opening of the back door—but one hundred wild cats and their kittens rush in if we do open it: they're fed later in the day and can seriously impede the art of cooking—to plunge us straight into a dream that every holiday brochure attempts to capture: sun; a young vine trained from the back door right along the pebbled path to Maria and Thodoros's house; geraniums that lift the heart with their wildly spreading profusion. Such a simple picture, which includes a chair on the tiles outside, a rush seat, the back and legs painted the ubiquitous Greek blue—but we're suckers for it, like so many millions of others.

So I can't resist going to open the door, to feel the blast of the heat, and to sniff, my first savouring of the day of the wild-herb smell from the mountains. This is the Greek Experience, we say, laughing at the 'Cousin Justin' attitude that adheres to Maurice Bowra, Cambridge dons and long earnest discussions of philhellenism. It's simple—though we know we'd be considered philistines—as simple as a blue chair and a bright-red geranium bush. And, here it comes: a black cat so perfect against whitewashed wall and red flower that it can only be found in the Greek islands.

It must be admitted that this landscape, for all our wild delight at sampling the 'Experience'—whether sitting high up at a taverna in a mountain village, sipping ouzo and picking at the ever-accompanying plate of *mezes* (little squares of feta, two olives, sometimes a tiny fried fish) that come unasked with the two-glass appearance of ouzo and fresh spring water, or picnicking in a sea of blue speedwell down on the flat sandy soil by the lagoon—doesn't really fit into the 'Greek' category at all. There is none of the bare, goat-nibbled mountainous landscape, which leads the traveller to mark out an olive tree, in the height of summer afternoon heat, and bask gratefully in its shade, knowing the next trees to be perhaps a good mile or so away. There is no sense of violent tragedy, as it is impossible not to feel at Mycenae, where Agamemnon's tomb leaves a chill that no amount of hot Peloponnesian sun can dissipate. Nor of ineluctable fate, like the sense at Delphi of the limits of the human freedom of will. Here, we are at the extreme edge of the Latin world. Despite the horrific grimace of the giant Gorgon found in a field south of Corfu town—from a temple dedicated to Artemis—it is easier to imagine the Romans here, than it would be across the narrow channel on the mainland. We are on a boundary; and the Turks, despite their enormous efforts to conquer Corfu (30,000 men, in the fourteenth century, landed on the north coast, and 20,000 Corfiots were taken as slaves), never established themselves here. To go back to Antony and Octavia, lazily wandering the Ionian, is more accurate an envisioning of history than the beys and pashas who ruled Janina over the sea in northern Greece.

The kittens, some white-and-grey-striped, some black and thin as pencils as they dart to the stove, smelling fish that Maria stews up for her family—fish brought in by Yorgos last night, bony, spiny and now submerged in hot peppers, tomato and oil—dance round our feet and drive us all out on to the platform of stone at the back of the house. We stand looking at the plants put there since the house was finished (and combining with the erection of the large rain-water cistern overhead). There are gardenias, which flourish in this corner sheltered from the *maestro* wind, and give off a luxurious, tropical scent; hibiscus, which add with their five-petalled peach and flame-chiffon blooms to the sudden impression of a Caribbean island garden; roses, which return the senses to England, pale and delicious-smelling, healthy in their Corfu habitat.

'If Kiria Paipetis comes, we shall have *sofrito*,' Maria pronounces. 'And pears in *krasi mavro*—with *yaourti*.' She looks challengingly at us, and we agree. The scents of the flowers, the insistent sun, which Maria doesn't seem to be affected by at all, and the clamour of the assorted cooking smells in the kitchen drive us indoors again. Thodoros, who is as quiet as his wife is ebullient and outgoing, but with the same Greek sense of humour as Maria (this is a trait that reminds me of the Scots, and leads me to believe there is a good reason why Scottish girls marry here frequently, only the mandatory year with the mother-in-law and the experience of village life sending them on occasions sharply back home), now walks up the last flight of steps from grove and beach. 'We shall have *sofrito* for Kiria Paipetis and her husband,' Maria informs him as he comes in, the cats and kittens rushing to clamber over his feet, for Thodoros is a soft touch when it comes to the cats—he loves them. 'I was saying that Dassia sings well,' Maria goes on, as Thodoros croons to the kittens: '*Na*-pss pss, *Na*-pss pss'; he finally settles on the blue chair with a swarm of the smallest on his knee. 'And now there is to be a band,' he informs us quietly. 'Dassia has said she wishes to play the trumpet in the new band.'

Sofrito (beef casserole, Maria's best dish) and pears in red wine vanish from our thoughts at the breaking of this news. A band! Maria had known, of course. There is even a rumour that my father is to be asked to be Vice-President of the band, and he has expressed delight at the notion. But the trumpet—Dassia . . .? 'I heard this,' and Thodoros gestures upwards to Liapades, the sign that indicates the source of all gossip, the centre of the world. 'Why not?' he asks reasonably.

But Maria can foresee difficulties. Suddenly, with pouting lips and furiously downcast eyes, she is indeed the oracle, she is definitely Greek and not Latin; she is, even, displeased. 'This may not be well liked,' are her final words.

We leave the kitchen; and as we go out of the back door a child from the village, released from the school in Liapades at the end of a long morning, runs down the last turn of the path and doubles back to reach the terrace. Of course! That was where Thodoros had been; not down by the sea at all, but up in the village, collecting the son of a friend or relative from school. Now it is time for the child to eat. Which will he have, I wonder: *keftedes* or the chicken made as it's made up there, and in villages all over Greece, by the secret recipe that is too simple to get right.

We, too, postpone our thoughts of the *sofrito* that will be lunch for the friends of my parents, a leading lawyer and his wife from the town. It's enough to walk down and look at the *Falaina* as she nods at the end of her rope by the new jetty, and plan to take her out later, or tomorrow morning in the early light. We return from the beach by way of the grove and the sunken garden, fantasising as we go on Dassia's coming success as a trumpet player.

'I can't see who would object,' I say. Everything seems so perfect here: it's the great mistake of the expatriate, I know, to assume that this bought happiness must belong to everyone in their chosen spot, but here I am, going in for it.

'You never know,' my mother says. She shows more knowledge than I do, as I'm later to realise, of the restrictions and demands of village life. Maria, who confides for hours at a time in so eager and sympathetic a listener, has clearly painted a startling picture.

But it does seem hard to believe in 'problems' and pleasures forbidden, on a day like this. Even the sight of Anna Georgiadis (whom I can never see without imagining the gold chains at her neck and wrists, hidden by the antiquated black cloth) doesn't deter me from allowing my spirits to soar. Anna, with her goats on the shingle down near the mouth of the cave, looks ridiculously picturesque (but I am the one who is being ridiculous, with my 'touristic' vision). The wild flowers glow like jewels in the long grass: grape hyacinth, purple mallow, the first poppies.

My son, with his friend Yannis, comes round from the side of the point in *Swift Swan*, his yellow rowing-boat. The sea is so calm we hadn't worried about them—and both can swim and row well. They dock the boat with expertise, up by the *Falaina*.

The sky is a perfect, unbroken blue. Even if we do have to go back home for my son's school in a few days' time, Rovinia will be here for us again when school breaks up.

My father, who has been painting high up behind the house where the seventh well is sited, comes down the grove to join us on the pebbles and sand halfway along the beach.

Although we don't have electricity yet, the success of the Colonel's last throw at finding water up on the hill at the back of the property has given him another rush of optimism. It does seem hard to believe that a year ago the house that stands behind us proudly, fifty yards above sea level and with its stoa of dark boulders of stone, was no more than a skeletal frame. Electrical conduits had been put ready, of course—and the pipes for the plumbing were all in the ground. But the house was uninhabitable—and now it is a joy to be in.

'Another lovely day,' my father says—although he has commented earlier that he's understood the lack of need to say this, out here, because every day is lovely.

And it is. What can possibly go wrong?

We're sitting at breakfast—my son and I, that is, for my father is down on the jetty with Thodoros, examining the engine of the *Falaina*, which is due to take us across the big bay to Alipa on the first stage of our journey back for the beginning of term, and my mother is in the kitchen with Maria, who is packing Rovinia olives in a jar, as a present for me to take to London—and the radio stands on the table between us. There is still no electricity, so the batteries are an important part of our shopping trips to town: without them the World Service, with its important, booming British voice, cannot be heard and the world will tick on without us knowing anything.

Today, however, we're both beginning to wish the batteries had gone flat last night and never been replaced. For that reminder of announcements on the 'wireless' in Scotland of the progress of the Second World War, which the self-important voice had broadcast when I was a child there, appears to have gone silent altogether—and, sinisterly, on every wavelength all we can hear is martial music.

At first we go on eating to the accompaniment of a brass band. Both of us are conscious that these are the last Liapades eggs we'll enjoy for some time; and we talk about Easter, and the eggs dyed pink and red, and the procession at the church that my son went up to, returning shining-eyed after midnight and calling out 'O Christos anesti' (Christ has risen), while cousins and brothers and sisters-in-law of Thodoros and Maria came in later, to reply 'Alithos anesti' (it is true he has risen). We had treasure hunts in the grove, with clues (not very good ones) written by me and then read aloud in translation to allow visiting children to take part.

Now, the innocence of Easter Day, the nests with their brightly coloured eggs in the crook of leaning olive trees, are suddenly being taken from us at speed. Thodoros comes up from the beach and goes into the kitchen, where their radio stands on top of the fridge and is liable to pour out Eastern-inspired music—or, as often, 'Never on a Sunday', which has become the theme tune of Greece, and which breaks for bulletins of gabbled (and incomprehensible to us) news. Today, there are none of these.

We leave for the airport, nevertheless. I go up to my room one last time; and, because I can sense all is not well—and because there are no foreign newspapers anywhere nearer than Corfu town and airport—I feel the need to *know* overcoming the wonderful timelessness of Rovinia. We are in the middle of something happening, that is clear; and for a terrifying minute I'm visited by the vision of the tortures and atrocities of invasions and war: the Romans, the Goths, the Italians, the French and the British have come and conquered the island of Corcyra; many have been killed, defending their country and their freedom. In the last World War the Germans almost succeeded in destroying the town and taking the island. Why should we, in this place of perfect peace and contentment, be spared the turmoil of history?

The trip to the airport is grim. (For me alone, I believe— well used to war, my parents seem unaffected by the significant absence of information, while Thodoros is as inscrutable as ever.) But Maria's goodbye hug had nearly reduced me to tears: if all is to change here beyond recognition, if this island and this house are indeed invaded or sequestered, part of an enemy chest of trophies of war, will we ever meet again? 'Adio sas,' Maria says in a tone considerably more hushed than her usual one—and, following us out to the top of the steps down to the sea, 'Kalo taxeidi' ('Have a good journey'), which seems, due to the tense atmosphere created by the silent radio, to suggest the expectation of an imminent descent into Hell.

The sea begins to get up when we're halfway across the bay, and spray drenches us, the water still cold from a long Ionian winter. Yet none of us, on this occasion, thinks to remark on this: it's as if, already, we're preparing for the reality of a new order, with all its risks and dangers. Those things that would only yesterday have been worth the worry—did I remember to pack a change of clothing for my son in our hand luggage, or will we have to rootle in the big suitcase after dragging it out on the beach at Alipa; did I put my London shoes in, or leave them in the dark recesses of the cupboard off my bedroom in the fast-receding house; will I have to travel with wet feet?—all seem totally insignificant now. And the sea, rising to the command of its ancient enemy, the *maestro*, rises and spits against the cliffs as our tiny caique, laden with people and luggage, makes its way round the point.

We glean the news at the airport easily enough. There has been a military coup. Our plane is late arriving from London—it may come, it may not—and if it does come it may or may not take off and go back there again.

I have to confess to cowardice. The jet *did* come in, many hours late, and sat on the tarmac, refusing to yield its intentions on the subject of the return journey. My anxiety grew to unbearable proportions. 'Yes, you had better both come back to Rovinia,' it was finally decided.

The next days, time out of school for my son, out of reality for everyone else, as Greece waited to hear what had pounced on it and snatched the country and its institutions, its politicians and protesters, up in its beak, are strange indeed. Suspended in the limbo caused by the takeover of Colonel Papadopoulos and his fellow-colonels, and without a telephone to connect us to the outside world, we rely on news from Liapades, brought down by villagers and the new pals we've made there. We drive to Skripero and try to phone 'home', as London still represents itself to us—but the queues in the post office make this impracticable.

'Home' begins to look more and more like the island of Corfu. Are we ready for this? Is our pose as home-owners, when we are actually no more than tourists, *xenoi* with a smattering of the language and an obvious delight in the 'Greek Experience', to be tested and then found wanting in integrity? Still, I am glad on two counts not to have taken that plane. We must learn first just how much of a risk it is to my parents to stay on here—and even though they show no sign of wishing to budge an inch, there is a good reason to be cautious.

In the Second World War my father was given a job by the then-fledgling SOE—the Special Operations Executive, which had been created to encourage resistance in countries that were occupied by the enemy. He was put into the department in Cairo controlling the mission to send trained agents into Greece and Yugoslavia to assist the resistance organisations with money, arms and explosives and to prepare Syria, Lebanon, Israel, Jordan and Iraq against the possibility of being occupied by the enemy. The position was a difficult one; for, while trying to help the resistance movement in Greece, he was hampered by the fact that Winston Churchill was determined to restore the King of Greece to his throne, and wanted Greece to remain a vitally important part of the Western world. The British wished to build up and assist resistance to the enemy—but the largest resistance movement in Greece was the Communist organisation known as the EAM—the National Liberation Front and its military force, known as ELAS. These movements not only harried the occupying German forces, but built up an effective government for the greater part of rural Greece.

We had heard the story before, of the small plane that left the mountains of northern Greece for Cairo in August 1943 with the leaders of the resistance movement on board.

Now, as we sit around at Rovinia, we ask to hear it again. The arrival at dead of night after a demand for consultation, this being gladly granted by my father; the meeting at which a recently appointed Ambassador to the Greek Government in Exile had appeared sympathetic to the Communists' appeals for assistance (they had already, between them, pinned down nine German divisions and caused them to have to fend off daily sabotage attempts and raids); and the final betrayal: the Ambassador the next day denying that he had even been there, when the delegation from EAM and ELAS came to Cairo. Worse still, the Communists were now, my father was told, in danger of arrest. After ensuring their safe passage on the small plane back to Greece, he flew to London, to find that his efforts to assist the resistance movements had gained him the sack.

'So what shall I do with the letters?' my father asks. Maria, laughing at my lack of resolve and my unexpected return to the house, is unpacking the olives she had given us in a big jar. There is a fortifying smell of *stifado*, the pork casserole dish we've come to enjoy almost as much as *sofrito*. (But will such pleasure still exist, for us or for anyone? And what indeed should be done with the letters of appreciation from the Communist leaders to my father, proudly kept in an old briefcase in a drawer of his desk?)

'There's always the floorboards,' someone says. 'You could put them under there.'

And we all sit silent, contemplating the dreadful

scenario of the colonels' henchmen arriving, and the ransacking of this house it had taken so long to build. In our mind's eye we see the ripping up of floorboards and even the plundering of the stoa, in search of evidence of this foreigner's wartime activities. What can be done?

One thing is certain. Summer term has begun, back in England. We go back, my son and I, by ferry to Brindisi, by train from Brindisi to Rome—and then to London by air. My parents stay behind in Corfu.

London is bursting and screaming with its new culture: Carnaby Street, the Beatles, drugs, and kissing and raving. No park is safe from the long-haired lovers, green men and girls who look as if they've become one with the flowers and trees. No street fails to resound to the whine of Bob Dylan. 'How are ya?' 'Hi.' 'Good' is called from room to room, corner to corner.

In the midst of all this passion for liberty and self-expression, it's hard to imagine the restrictions and punishing rules and regulations of Colonel Papadopoulos and his regime. Greece—birthplace (as the tourist books have it) of the democracy that students insist on in the Paris *événements*—silenced and curbed like this? It seems impossible. Reports come of grim island prisons, torture and thuggish methods of dealing with dissenters. There are fears for intellectuals and poets brave enough to stick it out in Athens, or indeed anywhere in Greece. The bright patina—it went with the Greek Experience nonsense (as it now appears)—of poetry and truth has rubbed dull and tarnished. What will my parents do, who have now given up their lives in Britain, if they find themselves at odds (a perfectly likely scenario) with the colonels? They'll come home, of course, but to what?

As I realise in that tumultuous summer of 1967 (tumultuous also because my own life has changed), there is no possibility that my parents would abandon Rovinia. It, and not London, is home to them now. They'll stick it out, and see what happens. '*Tha doume*'—we'll see—a phrase you hear ten times a day out there, sums up their attitude to this dreadful new development in the country they love. And '*dhen pirazei*'—never mind—seems to be the equivalent to their answer to those who fear for their happiness or safety. There are thousands suffering in the real sense, under the colonels; where Rovinia is, the same sense of timelessness and unchangingness still seems to prevail.

And, when I go back there, so it does. Rumours that all the colonels (or one of them, or two) have large villas on Corfu are neither substantiated nor found to be false. Spreading like rocket spray over a night sky, crazy tales come of hidden nuclear bombs in Nausicaa's Cave, just south of our bay, and of millions spent on arms by the colonels, some of these stored right here in Alipa Bay.

Within an hour of arrival, the pale-blue sea as it shades into emerald and deep ultramarine, fanning its magnificent tail as it courts the distant horizon, has caught me in its lure again. The sun sits incontrovertibly in the sky, and goes down over the Monkey's Head, as it always has done. The autumn equinox isn't far off, and we will see a crimson crown just over the ancient scar in the mountain that is a parting in the hair of the monkey. We shall sit on the terrace in the evenings and watch the sky warm to red, then purple, and then cool to blue/mauve. My father will take out the binoculars, and we'll look at Venus, which shines in cheap-bauble colours when seen through the magnifying glass. A shooting star will come down millions of miles distant and on top of us, all the same. The hoot of the scops owl (so say some) or the tree frog (in the opinion of others) will sound from the quiet hill opposite, where trees and scrub have melded into one barely visible jungle. The feeling that things have been like this for uncountable ages will be as strong as ever it was here.

Something new has come—or is about to come to us, though; and today we're standing in the port of Corfu where the big ships dock from Ancona or Venice, and the ferry from Brindisi discharges its tired passengers, the blurry eyes of all-night deck-sleepers suddenly revitalised by the glorious mountains and fresh air of Corfu.

We're walking away from the crowds and entering the world of smaller boats, each one standing at the ready and waiting for the next sea voyage, after cleaning and repairs have been completed.

We walk further on, and further; and there, as my father points and looks with pride, is the new caique he has had built, as splendid and strong as the large fishing caiques we see plying the oceans, from our vantage point on the side of the hill at Rovinia. 'We can go as far as the islands on her,' he says as we stand gawping at big *Falaina*, berthed quietly in the inky waters of Corfu port. He smiles, and indicates we should board. 'We'll take her home,' he says. 'Of course, there's no question of anchoring overnight in Rovinia Bay.

There's no protection from the storms, and they get up so quickly. But we can keep her over at Alipa—and drive there to bring her round.'

I have seldom seen my father look so pleased about anything, and it comes home to me that of course it's as a sailor that he sees himself. He knows about boats. And I can see his eye run with approval over the broad, sensible *Falaina*. 'A Lister engine,' he's saying as, hardly able to believe this is really us, we walk along the jetty and board the caique. 'She sails under the Red Ensign,' my father says.

To travel by boat to the west coast of the island from Corfu town on the far side is no short journey. We take the pounding of the waves as we round the northern coast, by lying on deck, feet braced against the rail. The *Falaina* pitches and rolls; and she ploughs through waves that look dauntingly high. But none of us wants to miss the spectacular experience of sailing halfway round Corcyra in our very own caique. And no-one admits for one minute to feeling even slightly seasick.

Below deck the *Falaina* has everything that might be required on future trips—to Paxos or Anti Paxos or Mathraki. There's a cabin with two bunks, a galley kitchen and a WC. The sense of sturdiness is maximised here, by the comforting width of the boat: you can imagine a big catch being hauled aboard and tossed down into the belly of the ship; and indeed, the *Falaina* follows exactly the lines and proportions of a fishing caique. It's just—perhaps shamingly—pleasurable to reflect that we and not a squirming net of mullet or *gruppa* will be the cargo; and that, Vangeli willing, we can go exactly where we want.

Vangeli is an indispensable part of the new *Falaina* life that is envisaged for Rovinia. A mechanic at Manessy's garage in the town, Vangeli is a tirelessly patient, clever and smiling man who likes to sail at weekends; he works at the garage during the week. Perfect, when it comes to going out for trips in the *Falaina*, for there is nothing Vangeli likes to do more than sail out over the wide sea on a Saturday or Sunday, and drop anchor by a shore where no trace of human habitation or settlement can be seen. The small *Falaina*, dwarf sibling of our new caique, will come along too on these excursions, towed in the wake of the big *Falaina*. Thus, if we come in somewhere where it's too shallow to find a mooring, we can transfer to the little boat and chug along a foreign coast.

The possibilities are intoxicating. Dazed, sun- and salt-burned, we totter off the caique (it's miraculously calm at Rovinia and we come right up to the jetty), observed first with suspicion and then with delight by the fishermen from the village who are tying their nets on the beach.

We fix up Sunday as the day for our maiden voyage. We'll leave at ten, with a picnic—from Rovinia if the sea is quiet; from Alipa if it's blowy. None of us can think of anything else; for the big *Falaina* satisfies that longing for a freedom to go across the sea that must live in every race on earth. Thodoros will be one of the party, and he will do some serious deep-sea fishing.

Sunday is 'another lovely day' (we still cannot resist remarking on the so un-British phenomenon) and we breakfast early on figs picked from trees up at the back of the property—and quantities of the small, purplish fruit brought by Thodoros from his own trees high above Liapades. Tea, coffee and a slab of bread with honey so rich and gold you believe the bees must have swarmed from Mount Olympus—or from the Attic hills themselves—to provide it. Grapes, the first muscats of the season. Why should the summer ever end?

The big caique, blue and white like her small replica, the little *Falaina*, sits by the jetty in water that can only be described as pellucid. Vangeli and Thodoros are standing together, talking: even though they're only a couple of inches away from each other, they shout, as all Greeks do on beaches; and when Yorgos the fisherman joins them, you'd be forgiven for believing a major row was going on, so developed are the acoustics here by the time you're fifty yards up the hill. In fact, they're probably discussing the fish Thodoros caught last night, taking the small *Falaina* down the coast to the south. There, an archaic figure in the boat, with a wall of virgin forest to one side of him and a great expanse of darkening sea on the other, he hooked a gigantic fish. I have to confess I don't know what it is, when I ask him and he replies, modest and quiet as he brings it into the kitchen in the now-enveloping darkness. Besides, there is a crowd collected already when he enters with this great fish—as if some piscine radar operates in communities by the sea, and all those whose livelihoods depend on pulling fish from the deep hear its signal and hurry down from Liapades to measure the new catch for themselves.

Today, as seems always to be the case in Greece, events

of the night before are utterly expunged from memory. There might never have been a collection of faces, lit by the overhead lamp in the kitchen, staring down at the huge fish, the starers' inescapable cigarettes filling the air with a familiar, eye-stinging reek. Someone put a fag (ironically, the most common name of the Greek cigarette is Papadopoulos, so the dictator much loathed on the island is constantly displayed by name to those who light up) in the jaws of a smaller fish, ignored by reason of its inferior size and also a part of Thodoros's triumphant excursion along the coast. '*Kapnize*'—it's smoking—someone calls out, laughing, as the wretched fish does indeed appear to be puffing on the cigarette. Luckily, before my own cry of dismay can be heard, Maria's rough and sensible hand has prised the weed from the fish's jaws and consigned it to the bin.

This minor farce-cum-tragedy has been forgotten, now that day offers its new drama of a maiden trip in the big *Falaina*. The mammoth fish brought in last night is no longer a denizen of the Ionian night waters, but a gutted, filleted monster in the deep-freeze in Thodoros and Maria's house in the village. (Liapades had electricity connected two years back; we still wait for the *Deii*, the gods of light, to come down to Rovinia.) The promise of more and bigger fish—as always, the fisherman's dream—shines out from the eyes of the men waiting on the pier as we go down.

It is almost impossible to describe the excitement of boarding a caique, especially one built to order and boasting the by-now-much-discussed Lister engine imported from England. My mother, a sea lover in every shape and form— she doesn't even mind the huge waves and angry winds that beat up the once-blue Ionian in winter—goes to lean ecstatically on the rail as we set out, churning up water that turns from emerald to dark tourmaline to an opaque blue that is almost black. My father, who sits in the stern, hand on the tiller, is speechless with contentment. My younger sister Catherine and I go to perch right up in the prow of the *Falaina*. We're high here, above a sea you practically feel you're sitting in when in the small boat; and only the knowledge that the little *Falaina* is coming along too, riding in our wake, makes us feel we'll be able to jump in and out of the water again, at our pleasure. Vangeli goes to sit by my father, and they shout to make themselves heard over the roar of the engine. Thodoros has his fishing line to prepare and clambers up and down from galley to deck. Oh—as we might say if we had a chance of being heard (for now, inevitably, a *sirocco* wind, the curse of these islands, the wind that blows up from North Africa, has come to try us, and Vangeli already shakes his head; should we worry? will we be plunged to the bottom of the sea?)—oh, for a Life on the Ocean Wave!

It soon becomes clear that being in a caique is the best place to be when a serious wind gets up. My sister and I crawl down to the cabin and gaze greenly and bravely at each other. Both our parents appear unmoved by 'the slight roughness', as my father puts it. And, when we glance out at the frothing stream of white that we leave as we chug towards the Dolpondia Islands, our destination for the day, we feel proud at the way the small *Falaina* is riding the swell. She prances, dives, rocks and sometimes almost disappears in the (to us) gigantic waves in this sea we've only been on when a ferry from Brindisi brought us over at dead of night, to Corfu port. We're proud of the little caique, her yellow and blue and white colours now, in our eyes at least, identifying her as one of our family, our fleet. If she can handle this, then so can we.

Mathraki is one island in this group of four, three of which are sparsely inhabited; Diabolos being the only one not settled. (The others are Othonoi and Ericoussa.) Most of the locals long ago emigrated to Australia or America. We're not going in to the small harbour, it emerges, but are going to drop anchor by a stretch of coastline where there won't be a soul in sight. We'll transfer to the small boat and go right up to the beach, then walk over the island—where, so we have heard, there was once an ancient settlement. We all picture the shards, even the fully formed clay pots, that will yield to our inspection, on Mathraki soil.

The wind begins to become gentler, and by the time the island with its low undulations (after spending each day looking out at the mountains from Rovinia, we can't even call Mathraki's hill a hill) has come into sight, our appetite has returned in every way. To swim: we jump down in barely disturbed water so clear the ridged sand is like shirred silk beneath an overskirt of cerulean blue; to explore: we watch as my father sets off eagerly in search of the remnants of neolithic Mathraki; to eat and drink: we eye the picnic box, so undesirable in rough weather and now, with the ice suitcase we have just the other day bought in the town, awaiting us temptingly below. We know we must swim and walk first, or we will indeed all sink on to that carefully nature-raked sand and drown in three feet of water. And the thought of the meal that's coming gives us energy, after the shaking we've had on our first experience of Life on the Ocean Wave. It's so perfect here, too—as yellow and blue and white as our invading boats. But then, with a cry of delight, my sister, swimming lustily to shore, discovers the mud. It's a free facial; a mud she remembers—calling back to me, spitting out the seawater and laughing as she rubs it across her cheeks, over the bridge of her nose and around her neck and shoulders—as being infinitely restorative. A beauty and health treatment, in one.

Later, as we sit on the big *Falaina*'s foc's'le and eat our picnic, we look at the flints my father has found on the low hill of Mathraki. These are arrowheads, surely—polished and the colour of a lizard's skin, brownish-grey, shining when rubbed against a trouser leg or with a kitchen cloth. The boat rocks gently, and we lay the flint weapons on the deck at our feet. Thousands of years ago, we say as my sister tries unsuccessfully to wipe off the mud on her face and chest, the people of Mathraki may have rubbed on this mixture, to frighten each other away, before shooting the honed blades of flint in war or in order to repel strangers. (But the mud, when it is finally removed, has had a good effect, and we talk of setting up a business and bottling it for tourists in the town.)

The picnic, the Boat Picnic as it comes to be known, is delicious: cold chicken, mayonnaise made from Liapades eggs and 'our own oil'—oil that is the province of Thodoros and Maria and which we receive from them each year, along with the olives of Rovinia (after the forty rinsings in salt water needed just as a beginning of the preparation). Then there's the rice salad, never more divine to the taste than when eaten on board the big caique, out on an expedition: tomatoes and strips of red and green pepper mixed with olive oil and lemon juice and added to the rice, served cold and glistening from its plastic box. And wine—has the ice suitcase proved a success? It has: the retsina is chilled, but not too much so. Water—it seems strange, to be drinking from our rainwater cistern when we're off the coast of Mathraki. 'Cheers' and '*Herete*' spill from us all as we toast the efficiency and stout reliability of the big *Falaina*. Time to pull up the anchor when we've all slept, on the shady side of the boat or down below in the suddenly covetable bunks. This, we agree, has been a perfect day.

Yet, like the Greek drama that so often divides a day out here into three acts, we are not finished yet with the story of the *Falaina*.

'Mirizei, mirizei, octopodi kai risi'—*the words of a wedding* song that proclaims the smell of octopus and rice, the traditional nuptial banquet, comes back to me as I survey the prospects for a long and probably very cold (it's November and the very end of the half-term) day ahead. The words were sung by Kiria Agirou, the energetic sister of Marie Aspioti, as she demonstrated, in floodlit tourist surroundings, the folkloric dances of the island on the occasion of my first visit—as a journalist—to Corfu. Would my mother, my friend Tim and I be eating *octopodi* and dancing, as Yannis wed—another of the many Yannises (most of the other men, not being John, are named after the patron saint,

Spiro)—while my son and my father, content with taking
his rowing-boat out on a glassy sea, enjoyed themselves at
home? Did we, despite gratitude at being invited and a gen-
uine desire to see what a Corfiot wedding would be like,
after the long wait between engagement party and marriage,
really have to go?

Certainly, we did. My father, who had gone up to a
funeral only a few weeks back (my mother being unable
then to accompany him), had come down the path wearing
a chastened expression: told to arrive at the widow's house,
he had waited several hours before finding himself in a
queue to kiss the medallion on the corpse's chest. The inter-
minable service in the church, half-hidden on the road up
from Yefira Bay to Liapades, had the men standing outside
on a day when the glories of October and sun on cyclamen-
covered hills were rapidly succeeded by a crisp evening and
lengthening shadows over the sombre cliffs painted by
Edward Lear. The coffin, still open, had been carried past
the men and into the church. All this was to be followed by
a long wake—and as the deceased had not been a friend, my
father had thought it possible to dodge back through the
olives to the house, forgetting, as he was inevitably bound
to do, that the twilit landscape held many observers, all
ready to report on the absence of '*o lordos*'—as my father,
equally inevitably, had now come to be known—from the
gathering.

Today there were stronger reasons for a show of solidarity
at the wedding ceremony and the succeeding feast. Yannis,
related to many in the patchwork of Liapades land, and
already a frequent visitor to the house (his friend Adonis is

building a caique with his own hands, which the two young men hope will take them far out into good fishing grounds), is marrying Katerina, the daughter of a neighbouring village family. Katerina, we have heard—but without surprise being evinced by the teller—is fourteen years old. 'She'll be asleep if the party goes on too late,' one of the women callers to the kitchen door announces. This is followed by a brisk discussion on the quantities of food ordered for the celebration following the ceremony. Rather like the bride's age, which seems hardly possible, the numbers catered for and the sheer weight of beef and salami already in preparation at the hotel built just above the coast road at Paleocastritsa, are quite astonishing. Surely, with the *mezes* as well, there cannot be a need for spaghetti? Like the juvenile bride, the wedding guests (we, at least) begin to feel an exhaustion coming down halfway to meet us. How shall we survive this ferocious hospitality? Will it be appalling bad manners if we flake out before the meat courses, fearsomely expensive and important as symbols of the grandeur of the occasion?

As it turns out, none of us need have worried, so infectious are the happiness and gaiety of all concerned. At three-thirty, precisely the time we are instructed to arrive, we present ourselves at the bridegroom's house; and the moment we are in the *avli*, the neat courtyard kept by Yannis's parents, we know we will not be seen as frighteningly 'different'; that we can just be ourselves and will in the end be considered as ridiculous or not as, say, Loukas and Petros, the near-identical cousins who have already arrived at Yannis's house and are drawing laughs as they describe too excitedly their recent (and some say invented) journeys to exotic and foreign climes. We're the equivalent of village idiots, I can't help thinking, as I catch the glances of the girls, none more than sixteen years old, as they scan my mother's and my denim skirts and other garb more suitable for the very young—in Liapades, at least. The difference is, we're idiots who have bought into the village; and the good-natured laughter from the locals has no malice in it at all.

Drinks, sweet and sticky, are downed. My friend Tim, who's at Rovinia for the first time, has a Metaxas cognac and we find that plates of cakes even sweeter and stickier than the liqueur are an essential element of the party. We watch Yannis, as he returns from his walk up to her house with the bride on his arm—and, along with the rest, we give out a loud cheer. What matter if little Katerina's school-friends double up with mirth at the sight of our faces too-soon pink with alcohol and the winter sun, which has had us swimming in the bay this morning? We're here to have a good time—and the bride, smiling and coming up to my mother to kiss her, seems well pleased to find us here.

The steep, winding main street of Liapades has seen many processions—and it's possible to see the road, as it twists and turns on its way up to the *plateia*, as itself the train of a bridal gown: for today, as people stand outside their doors or in the doorways of the grocery stores, pastry shop and ironmonger's, and a violinist precedes the wedding guests, the street itself appears to move, to shift lazily into the final stretch before the square with the tree, and with one last flick to deliver its burden right by the church door.

I have to confess to this being the first time I had been to a wedding in Corfu. Despite all the evidence of the extraor-

EMMA TENNANT

dinary (to us) laziness of Greek men—the long hours of sitting in cafés, playing *tavli*, or simply chair-in-street gazing while the women toil in the fields or work on building sites—nothing had prepared me for the disobedience, even wild abandon, of the men at a marriage service. For there is chaos in the church, as we see as soon as we go in. No-one, male or female, it immediately becomes clear, will take an allotted seat: everyone collects in the front of the church, where the poor *papas*, clapping his hands in vain, calls again and again for silence. The women do, in the end, sit down—but the men, shouting and wandering in and out right through the service, wouldn't dream of sitting or kneeling. After all, their yelling, milling presence seems to declare, why should they do what's required of them, when in life they are waited on and expected to stay idle? I'd seen the boy-children of women from the village who were working in the groves, as they ran at speed away from mothers who took an hour out from their precious labour to try and spoon-feed the already plump-kneed tyrants. If beseeched like this as boys, what chance was there for the men?

Despite all the clatter and shouting, we can just see the flowery wreaths as they are laid on the heads of bride and groom. We make our way as best we can to join the queue of people passing the couple as they sit by the side of the altar: like the rest, we press envelopes containing a money contribution into the hands of the bridal pair.

Dancing in the *plateia*, when the church is finally emptied of its noisy congregation, makes me think again of Marie Aspioti's sister, white-haired and dancing at the imagined feast she has laid on for tourists on the far side of

{ 131 }

the island. But—when the dancing is over and three hundred guests have piled into forty cars, hooting all the way down the hill and out of Liapades, hooting all the way to the hotel above the Paleocastritsa Road—I have to admit I couldn't manage the *octopodi kai risi* that Kiria Agirou sang of all those years ago. Maybe the fashions have changed and the old tradition—would Odysseus have been given octopus by his admiring hosts, if he had after all married Nausicaa?—has been subsumed by the modern need for show. For the feast was enormous: there were indeed *mezes* (which seemed to last forever, the little filo pastry triangles of cheese succeeded by fried whitebait, salamis and olives and feta, all washed down with ouzo) and then, just as we had been warned, came spaghetti, and after that huge sirloins of beef. Not to mention the wedding cake, tier after tier of cream and white icing.

We paced ourselves, we ate and drank—and, finally, we made our way back to the Yefira road and thence across moonlit groves to the silence of the house and a windless sea. The place feels empty and strange as we let ourselves in; and we're glad to be asked what the wedding of Yannis and Katerina was like. 'The men were impossible in church,' one of us says, and we all laugh—just as, very probably, the guests at the wedding party are now, in a friendly way, laughing at us. 'And the bride did fall asleep,' my mother adds. 'But after all, she's only fourteen.'

Coming down the hill from the village, it's possible to see what appears to be a Martian landing pad about one hundred yards down the precarious path to the point. 'People do seem to be rather wary of staying there—but in a way it's the loveliest place of all,' my mother says; and my father agrees. The fact is, however, that two elderly ladies, one a physiotherapist and the other the leader of a quiet, refined life in a Hampshire country house, have already stayed in the building known euphemistically as the Wing, at Rovinia; and both have been alarmed by the experience.

The landing pad, as one comes down nearer to home, finally reveals itself as the roof of a very small house, built just after the main structure of Rovinia and made way for, in the same fashion, by blasting the rock just beyond the stone plant-garden at the western extreme of Rovinia House. From where we sit—whether on the terrace, or under the verandah at the long table with its fluttering cloth anchored against the wind by metal grips—it is impossible to see this new addition to the property. Put up as a place to accommodate guests, its invisibility from mainstream life at Rovinia clearly appeals to young couples and to those who like to sit under its sloping roof and write or sketch.

It must have the most beautiful view on the west coast of the island. The cave is tilted romantically, like the set of an opera, from the vantage point of the Wing, and is glimpsed through the branches of a wild olive self-seeded on the pebble path down to the beach. The sea is much nearer here, and the elements altogether more demanding than in the house: factors, perhaps, that are conducive to the unease felt by those early visitors. 'It's like being at sea,' says someone who has come to stay and is placed in the furthest bedroom of the two large square rooms of the Wing. 'No-one would hear you, if you called.' And, while feeling that this isolation is exhilarating—the crash of the waves at night, the spectacular thunderstorms and the scrub, a tangle of cistus and prickly gorse, which threatens to come down over the small roof of the Wing and take it over altogether—it is also possible to see why it is frightening here as well. 'With the steps,' my father says by way of compensation, 'it will be a quicker way down to the sea.'

Steps, it's true, are dominating our lives by now. A new flight from the Wing joins the main progression of stone stairs and stretches of plain gravel or pebble mosaic; and the new flight runs parallel—screened by wild laurel and olive—to the public right of way to the beach. Sometimes, running down those very steep steps, there's a glimpse of tourists toiling down or up, like an escalator running to the same destination but at a different speed. The fishermen from Liapades, whose path to their boats and nets this has always been, come so early in the morning, however, when only the palest blue light comes through the thin cotton curtains in the bedrooms of the Wing, that the disturbed sleeper, already kept awake by surf, thunder or what sounds like tropical rain on the roof of this low-built cottage, wakes and never goes back to sleep again. All in all, the steps to the beach are not adequate compensation, for some, for living right over the sea—but for those who love it, the trudge of boots on small stones is further confirmation of the pleasures of island life.

More steps—these most useful to everyone at Rovinia—are now going in; and we are able, at last, to walk up a great flight of rough-hewn stone from the back of the house to the path to Liapades. We've cut out the loop, tiring to the feet and trying to the spirit (for it meant walking past Rovinia and then doubling back, going over a particularly rocky part of the path leading down to the far side of the Wing) and, psychologically at least, the journey to the twentieth century, in the shape of our car, now seems much shorter.

We're not drawing the line, either, at steps. Pebbles need to be amassed again—but, fortunately, interior decorators have not descended on our cove and removed these natural treasures, while visitors who come by taxi-boat for the day from Paleocastritsa and occasionally draw faces on the large, smooth white stones in which Rovinia appears to specialise, find when they return that the renderings of German, Danish or Italian compatriots have been washed away, and the sea has shifted the pebbles yet again, forming an endlessly inventive arrangement of shelves and beds and litters of stone and bright emerald glass.

We need more pebbles because a new path is to be made up the side of the hill covered by virgin forest. A cabin, almost derelict, stands on a terrace high up the hill and looks out through olive trees to the sea. Was this a home for someone once? We don't know; and the question didn't arise when the land changed hands. What is certain is that a well (in working order, stones very crumbly around the sides) stands on this ravishingly pretty natural terrace, long since left to run to ruin but retaining, in spring, enough traces of former care and cultivation to give it the look of a Mediterranean site for a house that would be beyond compare. 'We could do it up ourselves,' we all say—and those who find even the solitariness of the Wing too near civilisation are determined to do just that. But it's a scramble, to pull up through the scrub to this level, and dangerous too, though none of us likes to say so, due to the presence of snakes in ground so long undisturbed. 'We'll make a new pebble path,' comes as the obvious solution to the problem. And so we start on the job, from the patch beyond the small bridge that crosses the riverbed, as it coils up out of sight of the grove and then rises vertiginously through untamed jungle. Help is needed, to complete this winding path of mosaic up through the trees; but the thought of the hidden cabin and its outlook (so different, on the east side of the valley, from Rovinia's, with a green swathe of primeval forest as far as the eye can see, and then the bright blue of the Ionian under an equally blue sky, beyond it) is so appealing that it does seem worth going on with the construction of this snake of dull brown, purple and mottled blue stones.

The real snake we'd come across recently was just beyond our living-room window. It lay alongside its replica, the plastic hose used to water the plants; a trellis on which the strawberry grapes are being trained runs overhead. Maria points to the trellis—this running along the wall just under the small bedroom upstairs and, as we see, a perfect point of entry, should it so wish it, for the snake. '*Astriti*,' Maria says. '*Poli asximo*, very bad.' And she goes for the broom. She has in the last month knocked a snake or two from a favourite hiding place, under the chest of drawers in the living room, with the wooden handle of the brush. As she strides down towards the kitchen, the small but deadly reptile slithers away into an aperture in the rock at the far end of the stone-floored area created for pots and plants.

Crevices in the dynamited rock are already sprouting wild figs and an abundance of grasses and ragged robin; now, with the asp (for this it is) so well concealed, we wish the over-hanging cliff hadn't gone back to nature with such speed. 'There used to be a serum against snake bites in the fridge,' someone remarks uncertainly.

Caught by my ruminations on Cleopatra and the asps—did they come to her in a basket, hidden under figs; was there just one, or, over-egging the pudding surely, a whole family of asps? Did she press them all to her breast?—I resolve to check this out with the books in the hall, and so I miss the search conducted by Maria, broom handle aloft, a figure in a frieze like an avenging Medusa. If she catches the snake, I fantasise, she'll plait it in her hair.

As easy as forgetting joy or pain—and as quickly and easily recognised when they come again—are the sight and smell and light and shade of country untouched by modern agri-cultural methods; and even, as the 'magic valley' that we visit whenever possible shows us each time, untouched by anyone at all.

This is one of our favourite excursions, and today we plan to follow it with a delicious lunch. '*Volta!*'—a trip, actually Greek for a walk—Maria calls to us from the terrace as we toil up the new stone steps to the path, and '*Sto kalo*'—to the good—the greeting that gives courage to those setting out, a benign imprecation much needed when it comes to the hairpin bends and unmade roads that travel anywhere here demands. We walk up, pausing to look down at Maria's head and laughing face as they recede beneath us at the foot of the new steps; and we hear already (for there are no pauses in the Greek landscape; we may take time off to catch our breath, but the various dramas being played out in the village and down by the sea wait for no man) the footsteps coming up from the beach. Here is the yell of Yorgos, whose trumpeting voice is due to a lifetime of shouting over the din of the sea; here—just visible as we reach the gate with its crooked label '*Idiotikos*' (private), to which few pay any attention, particularly as there is a gap between the gate and the post that would allow a small mule or donkey access to the property—here a group of young and old Sunday strollers, and clearly known to Thodoros and Maria, are welcomed as they gather round the kitchen door. Who are all these people? We know we are blessed, not to have to worry in a place so exposed to possible thieves or evil-doers from sea or land. Thodoros and Maria can tell, without the need to take my father's binoculars from the Venetian chest in the living room and examine arriving strangers as they disembark, who is good and who is bad, in this neck of the woods.

We arrive at the village puffing and panting, and are glad to pile into the car. We edge down the main street of Liapades, as ever narrowly missing the dangling legs of black-clad women on their beasts, and go slowly down the small road that leads out on to the main road running from west to east across the island. We go straight over the small cross-roads—whouf!—there's always a feeling of escape, of delight at the freedom of setting out with only Corfiot dogs determined to run under our wheels, and lorries backing out from hidden gravel pits, to slow us down.

Our route takes us to Troumpetta, a village slung so high

on the mountains that it looks down both sides, to the mountains of Albania and back at our own Italy-facing coast. But to reach this eminence is to crawl like a bug on a switchback: the coiling road, with its heady plunges, first from one verge and then the other (all these filled with the great silvery fronds of the tops of olives) and the precipices and potholes, each danger spot marked, so it appears, with a shrine to St Spiridon, fill up the best part of an hour. By the time we're up in the clean, much cooler air of Troumpetta, we feel as if we've been subjected to a funfair mirror-land of Disney proportions. The olive trees are so immense and gnarled that they seem more like the fairy-tale illustrations of Arthur Rackham than real trees that give sustenance to the local population. Yet here and there—one boy calling out to us from the side of the road, basket held out to tempt us (but we dare not look, for fear of distraction from the route), and one woman walking with her small daughter— people give the lie to the sense of fairy-tale unreality.

Now, from this great height, we begin to come down, ears popping. We take the road east to the great mountainous region of Pantokrator; and fork right for Roda. Then, a few miles on, we take a sharp right to Valanaion. The road becomes rougher and rougher—it's not a track, it's still a road, but wild flowers too rare to be seen normally by a roadside are noted and we stop several times to peer at them— and as we go further and further down, we get that rush of recognition that comes with each visit to the magic valley.

Theories that Impressionist painters suffered from myopia—this the reason for their hazy, uncertain pictures of a rural world about to vanish for ever, a last, misty glimpse of a pre-Industrial Revolution European way of life—are forgotten, in this hidden valley under Valanaion. The trees, whether holm-oak, chestnut or olive, with their feathery branches, do actually look like the trees painted by Renoir or Van Gogh. Because they haven't been pruned?—we cannot know. And the fields, as we descend the last stretch of the by now almost-path to the little hump-backed bridge over the stream, are a dazzle of meadowland as nature intended it to be: a bright, inviting green (though to lie down here would be to feel the sharp stones under the orchids and clover and wild jonquils and camomile) and yellow from coltsfoot bright as gold coins dropped from the sky.

Beyond anything else, this valley exemplifies the adage that in Corfu it is spring all year round. We lean on the bridge and see clumps of snowdrops along with cyclamen and marigolds. There is an old ruined farmhouse behind us and we wonder why a pair of trousers, quite new-looking, hangs from a string between two apple-trees in the overgrown yard. Why is there an orange cat on the windowsill of the roofless house, so calm and complacent it pays no attention to us? Is there someone living in this deserted place after all?

There is no answer; only the sound of the brown water, like a Scottish burn, as it goes fast and then more cautiously round the stones where a family of turtles were seen last time we came here. There is a silence, apart from the rushing, dawdling water, which something in us can't fail to understand and know—perhaps from childhood, possibly from an earlier age. This is the magic valley; and we hope it may remain as it is, undisturbed, for ever.

Now it is time to go on to Strinilas. We sit in appreciative silence as the car takes us up and up this time, away from the valley and on to the majestic mountain of Pantokrator. This time we're really climbing: the flowers at the sides of the road become small and alpine, the mountain becomes limestone, white, bare and jagged, as we go up through the last turnings to what must surely be the top of the world. There can't be human habitation up here—it's just too bare, rocky and inhospitable—yet, as we come into Strinilas, we know we're arriving at one of the most welcoming and hospitable villages on Corfu.

A huge elm tree dominates the *plateia* of the tiny village; and as the whole settlement is built on a slope, the ancient tree with tables set under it seems to lean downwards, an effect that somehow presages the feeling we expect to have after enjoying our meal at Strinilas. We drive past one taverna—probably excellent, but we are sold on the Oasis, a huntsman's taverna, its walls hung with guns—and park alongside the inn, where a fire blazes in the autumn months and where in summer you can choose to eat either in or out, under the elm tree.

We choose the long room, for it's just right in there and spring has still not turned to summer. The owners, a young man and his wife, who are both possessors of eyes of a startling gentian blue, describe to us the charcoal-grilled chops, sheep's cheeses and (always welcome) *xoriatiki* salad that they are offering today. We drink ouzo and the rough red mountain wine that goes so well with the grilled *souvlaki* and tiny chops. The cheese, so subtle a taste that we find it impossible to describe, is eaten first, rather than after this perfect meal.

By the time we leave the village we are indeed leaning

slightly downhill, and the negotiation of the road home is
very slow and careful.

I'm in the small Falaina, *going across the sea from Alipa, the*
harbour safest for caiques in stormy weather; and it certainly
is both cold and stormy, early April and about nine months
since my previous visit to Rovinia.

In that space of time, almost unbelievably (though to
Maria it is no great surprise: pregnancy and childbirth and
death are closer to the consciousness of women here, and
come and go with the regularity of the seasons and harvests), I have had a daughter, born eight weeks ago, in Feb-
ruary. She lies in a Moses basket in the half-cabin of the
small boat, in order to avoid the copious lashings of freezing
seawater that come in as we repeatedly hit the waves. I was
last in the hot sun here, I tell myself, as I huddle in a rain-
coat and my mother dumps an extra sweater on to the baby's
crib. I remember the red-and-white patterned silk dress with
the long-stemmed green flowers on it that I wore last July,
before taking the ferry to Brindisi and then going north,
feeling increasingly nauseous, to Rome and then Paris and
London. My son, now ten, accompanies us on what is a serious family undertaking, a visit to the roadless, phoneless
house where we must ensure that the baby doesn't come
down with any illness (though I know the doctors here in
rural Corfu are amongst the best you can find: they are the
youngest and most recently trained and are sent to far-flung
villages to gain experience).

For all that, there *is* something daunting about the

remoteness of Rovinia. 'The *Deii* are coming next week,' is the answer when I ask about electricity; but, thinking of the fickleness of the gods, I sense these longed-for technicians merely play with our hopes and emotions. Why should they ever come down to the house and transform our lives, ending for good our paraffin-lamp and candle-lit existence? What must we do to persuade the all-powerful *Deii* to visit us?

We arrive and stagger up the beach with the nappy-laden luggage and the baby's basket. The house seems a long way up, this time round; and a light but stinging rain falls, causing our feet, already wet from slithering off the jetty into shallow water, to slip on mosaic pebbles and lengths of gravel path alike. At the top, Maria bustles us into the house, where we're thankful for an olive-wood fire burning with a healthy crackle and glow; and we lift the sleeping child (her cheeks are very pink, but the sea crossing seems to have done her no harm at all) from the basket and lay her down on a cushion by the hearth. 'There's a road down to Yefira now,' my father says, as I ponder for the hundredth time the decision to come and live here. 'And they're building a hotel in the bay; a pity really, but it was bound to happen.'

Coming by boat has made me unaware of the real developments in the locality. A road down to the neighbouring bay of Yefira means that our car can be left by the verge, and the walk across olive groves and down the rocky path to the house is considerably shorter than going down to Liapades. A hotel, however unappealing the purists might find a structure going up in one of Edward Lear's favourite locations, will mean access to a telephone—and even to a bar, which could produce some of the night life so glaringly missing, for the young, at Rovinia. 'And the *Deii* really are coming, on Monday,' he adds, seeing me edge up closer to the fire, welcome but inadequate in such a large room, especially a room with french windows on two sides. 'Central heating,' I say, knowing myself to sound lily-livered—but the baby, surely, could do with a little warmth. 'Yes,' my father says happily. 'We'll need a transformer. It comes by boat on Monday as well—Thodoros will pick it up in the caique.'

The next days are about as cold and unyielding as a Mediterranean spring can be. Radiators, put in so long ago at the time of the building of the house, will actually give heat!—I check my premonitions to see if this can be true (they're not encouraging; and, as I discover, are on this occasion accurate)—and, rather than bath the baby in the blue plastic washing bowl that we bring in from the kitchen, along with kettles of water boiled on the Calor gas, we will actually have hot water in the bathrooms and shower. 'This is the season when the hotels are full of students,' Maria informs us; and she adds, laughing, that they're used to 'dry out the beds', after winter. In the Wing, where we sleep at first, I feel like a hundred students—for all the hot-water bottles ever made would fail to take away the dampness from the sheets. Finally—at least it feels drier there—we move into the main house and, still wrapped in cardigans and scarves, await the visit from the gods.

On the appointed day they come, four young men with ruddy faces and olive skin, excellent manners (Maria rewards them with giant mugs of Nescafé) and assurances that their poles will all be in the ground within a very short time.

Time may be as hard to measure for a Greek as distance. After hearing Lawrence Durrell's assertion that to ask a Greek how far a place is, is to be told in cigarettes—'one or two cigarettes away'—I begin to believe that time must be measured in a similar fashion. It isn't that the *Deii* smoke: more perhaps that, as gods, they expect the smoke from our sacrificial offerings to waft to their nostrils as they stand high on the grey wooden poles, affixing the electric cables. The sacrifice they want from us, in fact, is that we should not show impatience with their progress. My parents are extremely good at exercising patience; I am not, and never have been. And so it is I who feel annoyed with myself, when on arrival in the small caique all the way from Paleocastritsa, the transformer seems to take an inordinately long time to get carried up across the shingle and thence up our sea steps to the stairs behind the house. Everything takes its time here and there is no point—and certainly no courtesy—in hustling and hastening what is ordained to take a mysteriously appointed number of hours, no less and no more. I wander into the kitchen as the heavy steel box, about three feet by two, is hoisted to sit atop a pole near the summit of our steps leading from the back of the house to the path. I decide to lift the lid of the casserole, where the *spanakorisi* (translatable only as spinach rice), a dish that is close to a risotto but moister, almost liquid (and delicious eaten with the local Gravyera cheese), is simmering gently. Maria begins to tell me that tiny artichokes, only this size and with edible choke in the spring, have been spotted at the market in the town.

Boom! A loud bang interrupts her lecture. We look at each other for a fateful second and collide on the way to the door. The story of the artichokes and a dish that is known as *stin poli* (from the town) vanishes from our minds. The bang, I know as I race towards the steps, means the end of the prospect of central heating, for some time at least.

Indeed it does. Overloaded, the transformer simply blew up as soon as the (now shame-faced) gods connected it to the mains.

'Boom!' we say, as we stand on the terrace by the end of the balustrade that faces out directly to the sea. The small caique is making its way back to Paleocastritsa with the electricians and their burnt-out steel suitcase, Thodoros at the helm.

Somehow, I do not ask Maria when I return to the kitchen for the end of the artichoke story, how long it will be before the men come back.

You forget every time that Corfu is a province of the sun. It comes just when the showers and bright interludes of early spring seem to have set the scene: it comes like a thump between the shoulderblades, a crown of heat that sends us scuttling to the dark, tiled room off the hall to dig out straw hats. Resembling mad kings in Shakespeare plays, we walk the terrace in headgear twisted and broken by last year's casual use, straw sticking from the fraying rims, once-prized sombreros suitable now only for a donkey to wear.

No matter if the new brightness makes the eyes squint, and plunges the shade of the sunken garden into a pond of blackness where the lemons on the tree hang like expired lightbulbs. The presence of the sun is alluring, addictive, and we all court it in our different ways. My father sets off up through the grove, camera in hand, to capture a picture of the dance of purple honesty under the great tree at the top of the most ravine-like slope in the path. My mother, more Greek than any of us, still cautiously garbed in winter skirt and sweater, clips the white roses down in the garden and weeds the long grass to reveal the pale glow of irises. I sit on the terrace; the baby sleeps away from the sun, but near the incessant, reassuring home-making sounds of the swallows; and my son is far out in the small caique, fishing with Thodoros.

By the time the electricians come again, and master the giving of light and heat to Rovinia, the sun has supplied us fulsomely with both. We are grateful, but we don't need radiators any more: the days and evenings have warmed and there's enough of a nip in the air at night to make an olive-wood fire very welcome. We're beginning to swim, though; and it must be admitted that, for some of us at least, a hot shower is more than a luxury after braving water still cold from the long winter.

The sea—as we make our brief, heroic strokes through the freezing (so it seems to us) turquoise china plate that lies peacefully in the bay, ready to serve its entrants with shells, nostrils full of salt water, and the occasional glimpse of a kingfisher if you swim out to the rocky end of the point—is nevertheless preparing for a spectacular storm. Thodoros says this as he brings the small caique into the beach and my son jumps out into the water. '*Poli asximos kairos*'—very bad weather: it's odd to hear this when the sun makes the sea so inviting, and is hot enough already to make the head glad that the rest of the body is taking a cooling dip. What can he mean, when sky and sea, in a perfect concordance of blue, lie side by side on the horizon, straight as lines in an architectural drawing? There isn't even a whisk of a miniature pony's tail, when it comes to white horses, or spray against the cliffs under the monkey's pate, where the lighthouse blinks patiently, unconcerned with forecast or prophecy of doom. What can Thodoros mean?

The day goes on getting hotter and hotter. Greece has entered our blood by now, and we can no longer remember the cool summers back at home or the precautions taken when embarking on a picnic or a day by the sea: waterproofs, cardigans, rug that may never be unrolled due to sudden, half-expected rain. We all belong here now. The baby wears a white hat, which sits at a drunken angle on her dark-turning-to-fair hair. Most of us have gone bright red, but a tan creeps along arms and settles over freckles on the most light-skinned of the party. Even my mother changes to a fresh blue linen skirt and white shirt, a crisp triangle of cotton tied as a scarf on her head. We learn not to sit too long in the rays of this precious, free commodity; for to come up from the beach and linger too long on the terrace is to court stupor and migraine. 'The sun is stronger than you think,' my father warns visitors and even, sometimes, the first sun worshippers on our beach.

In the early mornings, as we have just begun to discover,

the small cove under the rock where the point comes down—a spot protected from the rest of the world by the overhang, and thus much desired by us and by incoming tourists alike—now has a new occupant; and one who keeps any other would-be bather away. After three or four years of a distinct demarcation line between the tourists and the locals—the latter, for instance, never came down to the sea to swim, except (and then only a few of them) in the heat of August—a pair of feet have been seen, sticking out on the pebbles, their owner obscured by the rock jutting out on to the beach. 'What can it be?' a friend staying at Rovinia asked innocently the day after her arrival, as if she had failed to recognise that toes were part of our marine land-scape. 'I couldn't think what this man was doing there . . .'

The toes belong to Alexandros, an old man with a piece of land in the patchwork on the way up to Liapades. He lives in a cabin, and is thought strange by the inhabitants of the village: '*trellos*' (mad), Maria says, tapping the side of her head. She enjoys the presence of the crazy old man on the beach below the house, though: his lying there stark-naked from the hour the sun rises over the bay until late in the evening is a symptom of the influence of an increasing num-ber of package-holiday visitors. If they can strip down to the tiniest of bikinis and loincloths, why on earth shouldn't Alexandros, a land-owner of the area after all, do as the Ital-ians and Germans and lobster-boiled British do—even if he's the only one who has, as it were, gone the whole hog?

We're back up at the house from our swim. The old man on the pebbles pays no attention whatsoever to us, nor does he acknowledge the presence of the taxi-boat men—all of whom he must know well—when they bring their new cargo of tourists to the beach. We've stepped gingerly past him: he is so white and old, the crazy man, that he resembles a cuttlefish, a scaly creature without breath, as he lies there silent in the full glare of the sun. 'Greeks never sunbathe,' Marie Aspioti concurs, when we tell her of this new development at Rovinia. 'They like to be private, not to expose themselves in the way you describe.' But I can't help thinking that maybe old Alexandros considers himself alone, in this bay that is entirely deserted early in the day. He is, at any rate, '*idiotikos*', as the word perhaps meant at its inception: private, but also mad to desire to exist in such a state.

The day continues as hot and lovely as ever. It's Saturday; the barometer in the hall has its needle on the 'e' of CHANGE, but there is no sign whatsoever of the bad weather we've been warned to look out for. We all, as we sit at the long table on the verandah, see the big caique in our mind's eye, down at the stone pier where a tourist boat waits for the stunned bronzers now staggering, carrier bags in hand, across the shingle to the jetty. 'Wouldn't it be a good day to go out in the big caique—on Sunday?' someone says. 'If it's fine tomorrow, of course.'

My father, a sailor, shakes his head. It's not only the certainty of the fishermen and Thodoros of the coming storm that deters him from setting in motion a trip with Vangeli and the big fishing-boat. His own instinct is pretty unfailing; besides, we have the barometer to aid us when we need to make decisions of this kind. Made by the delightfully named Negretti & Zambra, in London, this weather clock is consulted more often than the carriage clock on the table in the living room, which gives us the time. We live by the changing weather here; and the 'e' of CHANGE is just as undependable as it sounds. We could, as a result of its gyrations, find that we were left to sink or swim.

In the night, the storm begins. We're grateful not to have planned to take the big caique out the next day. What we still don't know fully, perhaps, is that there are some storms even the most practised sailor on these seas cannot foretell. It's in one of these, in the summer of a later year, that the big caique is caught out at sea.

It's hard to tell Petros and Loukas apart, when they stand down on the beach and argue; and by the time they've come up the steps and settled down outside the back door it's no longer possible to give them the equivalent of the Greek stare: for they really are, as my father said of my ten-year-old son and his new mate Yannis, 'as like as two peas in a pod'.

Loukas came back to the island only last year, after an eighteen-year stint in America. Despite this, he has the thickset body, slow-moving black eyes and hair that looks as if it's been thrown from a distance and gone hit-or-miss on the head, of his cousin Petros. A blade-thin roll-up is attached to his lower lip in exactly the same place as Petros's dangling fag; more arrestingly, both men have the same way of brushing their cheek as they speak, as if dismissing an eternal fly. Yet Petros has never, as far as anyone knows, left Liapades. Loukas, once a merchant seaman, speaks of New York and Central America with the insouciance of a professional traveller. The men's stories show them to be very different, when it comes to love and ambition—Loukas lofty in his aims, Petros tied to the demands and expectations of the world he has grown up in. They had certainly not met or corresponded during Loukas's long absence on the far side of the world (as America, desirable and unattainable, still appears to many in Greece) and yet, sitting next to each other on the rickety chairs by the back door, mops of hair identically skew-whiff and invisible insects perpetually thumbed from their cheeks and chins, it's as if there has never been a parting and a forgetting.

Maybe, as we hear more of Petros and Loukas, the answer lies in the sameness of their destiny: the question, of course, lies in whether either could possibly have known what lay in store for them all those years ago, before Loukas went away and the old men up at 'White's Club' in the village slowly erased him from their minds. Had it been clear to Loukas that the sole chance of avoiding his fate (indeed, the fate of many of his peers in Liapades also) lay in leaving home and going to the States? Did Petros, so accepting of his life, know all along that there was little point in fighting the inevitable decline? (Yet not all, of course, went downhill with the gathering speed of Petros and Loukas, both now fishermen on a coast denuded of its piscine harvest.) Was there some family insistence—some here might say a curse, an early offence committed against St Spiridon perhaps—that had brought about their descent from prosperity and the dwindling of their prospects, as far as the getting of a bride went, at any rate. Most of all, do they care?

The sun is setting on an evening like so many others, puce and vermilion over a sea scattered with colour like a sliced-open pomegranate. I am sitting on the stone balustrade, at the point where it curves round the western end of the terrace, the prow of a ship that was built by my father and mother when they still were not sure if they would live here—when London and the chilly North had to be home. I wonder, as Petros, closely followed by Loukas, comes out by the fig tree at the end of the terrace before it sidles down past the kitchen and under the trellis with the healthy young vine, how anyone can really know what they will do and where they will go; and, despite the banality of the thought, I turn to gaze right out across the ocean, as if I could catch Loukas's vanished eighteen years abroad there. The old men at the *cafeneon* in the village have died, since he returned, and their sons, as dependent on the working mothers, sisters and wives of the village as their fathers had been, are sitting long at the tables set with *tavli* and breath-clouded glasses. If they think of Loukas, it's as 'the American', although he'll never go back there. He'll be a millionaire for ever in Liapades, even if it's clear he has no money at all. Petros, who has never been away for as much as a day, is more invisible to the people in Liapades than his cousin ever became. He has never boasted, never departed and returned; only his folly is clear to the old men at White's, his naivety transparent.

Petros started off in life, as we have been told—but always with the chuckle that accompanies the relating of a coming misfortune—as an owner of a good many olives in the groves behind the valley where Rovinia was placed by my father and mother. No-one talks in terms of *stremata* (acres) here: 'quite a few olives,' they say, pointing uphill to

Petros's former inheritance. 'Then he began, bit by bit, to sell them—yes, it wasn't long before he'd sold nearly all the olives up there where you're looking, just a little to the *aristera* [left]; yes, over by the rocks. Petros wanted a caique. Yes, with the money he bought a caique.'

I watch the two men as they amble back to the chairs where they've been for an hour now, the sunset seen and recorded. (Possibly, it seems to me, if you come from this technicolor-evening scene, it's an occurrence that deserves a respectful nod, each time. I try to imagine a childhood under a sun as violent and many-coloured as the Greek sun, and fail.) 'So what happened with Petros's caique?' I ask each time the subject of him comes up. I like to think of him in those now long-forgotten days at the helm of a splendid fishing-boat. Surely, if there are fish left to catch, Petros would be the one to catch them. For, like Loukas, he is muscular and strong. He walks more slowly now than he did, no doubt, but his gait may be due to his astonishing succession of mistakes, all easily avoidable, which people love to recount. 'He sold the caique and bought a smaller caique,' goes the story. 'And the foolish part is that he sells in winter, when no-one wants to buy a caique, and buys in the spring, when the prices are high.' 'And then?' I ask, although the evidence of Petros's increasing silliness lies down on the beach below us. The punchline, when it comes, is delivered with gusto. 'Now Petros has only—' and arms go akimbo in the rowing position.

Just as darkness falls, I go down the steps and walk across the shingle to the cave. Somehow, unseen in the gloom, Petros has got down here first; and he stands by his dinghy, final evidence of his disastrous business sense. There are few catches for this fisherman, who once was the proud owner of precious olives up the hill; and in the dark the little boat looks no bigger than a child's collapsible craft.

Loukas has long since disappeared in the opposite direction, up to the village. As Petros drags his small boat up on timbers left by Yorgos earlier in the day, Loukas will be arriving at the main square of Liapades. They'll look up for a second or two, the men who have inherited the story of Loukas, and then resume their play and their drink. For Loukas, who has come back from America—so everyone says, at least—with a fortune, has bought himself a taxi and yet, mysteriously, has not done well. As poor as Petros now, and without even a boat of his own, Loukas goes out to fish with those who let him. The taxi, rusting but still serviceable, can be seen in use on the occasion of weddings or funerals in the village. For all that, 'the American' has phantom riches still, and his stories are believed by Adonis, Petros's younger brother—he who became engaged to a pretty village girl, but lost her when he boasted that he would fly in his own plane on their wedding day, 'round and round'. So, all three, Loukas and Petros and Adonis, can be seen early in the morning and at dusk, as they put out and come back from the empty sea.

The Greek side of my father—he now eats the infamous skordalia (the Garlic mash which, served with roast chicken or fish, gives a pungency to the dish unimaginable in past days in Scotland)—is also expressed in the increasing friendliness of encounters with those from Liapades, and even with tourists who come up from the beach and ask urgently for the lavatory. White hair by now resembling a slipped halo below a pate blushing pink from the Corfu sun, he resembles a St Nicholas who has strayed, much to his own delight and surprise, into a Mediterranean landscape for which a cold northern upbringing failed to prepare him. Each day is a cornucopia of wonders: a new light, perfect for trying to capture in oils, is spotted on a simple expedition to a neighbouring village; wild flowers, especially the clouds of purple honesty and the poppies that bloom unseen under olives or down on beaches unreachable by man, fill him with spectacular joy. And, just as much as the old habitués of 'White's Club' in Liapades, who call out their *Kali mera* and *Herete* with resounding enthusiasm as he goes past, the sunburnt Swede or boisterous Italian who rushes up the steps, unheeding of the fading PRIVATE sign by the high-water mark, warms instantly to my father's so-evident happiness.

Yet, this time when I arrive with both my daughters, the younger of them three, I note that my father is no longer happy. My mother, making every effort to control her feelings, is also disturbed. Their faces lighten when Rose, the three-year-old, says firmly on embarking on the *monopati* down through the groves, 'I like it here!' But it's sadly the case that something is making both my parents decide they're not liking it here at all. My father's wave to Yorgos as he comes up from the beach is, for the first time, almost perfunctory. He shakes his head when Yorgos tries to engage him in the nonsensical English-Greek conversations they

usually both enjoy. With a disturbed expression the fisherman shuffles down to the door at the back by the kitchen.
Here a gloomy silence reigns—despite the fact that it's Saturday, and Thodoros and Maria's son Spiro, now seven years
old, usually rushes around the terrace and house, followed
by a laughing troupe of callers to the hospitable Rovinia.
What on earth can have happened? Is this a seven-year
itch, for my mother and father? It must be about that length
of time since the feast in the grove beneath where we now
stand, to mark the roof being set on the structure of the
house. Has there, improbable though it seems, been a
change of mind about the whole venture? Do they no
longer wish to live here at all?

We have the whole of the rest of the day to find the
answer. The joy of rushing down to the sea and losing all
vestiges and memories of the aeroplane, followed by a car
journey in the blazing sun behind a tourist bus bound for
the monastery at Paleocastritsa, can never be extin-
guished. But the pleasure of the first ouzo and the satisfaction in the initial handful of black olives—then the
ensuing declaration from all concerned that this is the best
crop yet from the trees here—aren't as marked as on previous occasions. Is it inflation perhaps—we're in the mid-
1970s and Greece is caught in its throes. Do my parents,
who have put nearly all they have into this house and this
life in Corfu, now find they can no longer afford it here? Is
this the last sizzling plate (heated by Maria to an untouch-
able degree, but rightly so, for even in summer a gust from
the *maestro* can cool food and plates alike in two seconds
flat) of *bouti*, the leg of lamb cooked with rosemary from

the huge wild bushes by the steps, and blackened onions, with green beans and *kolokithaki*, courgettes, to accompany it? When, if ever, will we be told the reason for this new unease?

The answer has an ironic twist—for what it is spells out the word 'satisfaction', while pinpointing my parents' now almost total lack of it.

It's dark earlier—always quicker than we expect, those of us who come from the long, grey twilight of London—and we're sitting at the table on the verandah for dinner and an inky blackness, punctuated by the hopeful peeping of the owl in the trees opposite, wraps us round like a warm shawl. A candle flickers, throwing shadows on the rose-and-white pattern of the tablecloth. The wine, great flagons of retsina and red, which sell in the town for a sum not connected with present inflation—one pound or less, for a two-litre bottle—is being drunk when the sound first comes in to us across the water.

I admit the extreme heat of the evening had led me to suggest that we did what the real summer weather some-times dictates, which is to move the table out to the front of the house. Here, among my mother's pots and plants, and head-on to the sea, the occasional breeze is greeted with the delight accorded a long-awaited guest. Under the verandah, in these stifling conditions, it can seem claustrophobic in the sweltering August weather.

I'd made my suggestion while light still lingered over the bay. My father, usually pleased to be able to look down from his Olympus to the shore, where he has placed lights that glow magically around the mouth of the cave, had appeared

distracted and made some excuse not to move. By the time
we had embarked on a salad and a dish of whitebait, the reason for his desire to find as much protection as possible at
the side of the house became only too clear.

The sound, indecipherable at first but horribly, echo-
ingly loud, is music from the new hotel built on the mountain that runs along beside the Monkey's Head; a majestic,
crude block of darkness that forms the principal view from
Rovinia when looking out to sea. As if to taunt those coming to the island as we did, before any development took
place, both an international airport on the east of the island
and the white modern honeycomb hotel above Paleocastritsa had appeared shortly after Rovinia went up. Of
course, no-one had complained at the arrival of either. It
would have been madness to expect to obtain a view as wild
and untouched as ours had been for much longer in an
already overcrowded Mediterranean. The absolute and
unchanging purity of the sea was, and remains, a miracle.
And a new airport brings revenue to the island's population:
tavernas, new hotels and 'Rooms' had begun to go up. So
the white blotch against the black-brown flank of the
mountain went tactfully uncommented on. But the introduction of a nightclub—'a disco', as my father said in deter-
minedly neutral tones—was certainly a disaster.

'I can't get no satisfaction,' booms Mick Jagger across an
expanse of water as smooth and polished as an old-time
ballroom floor. The speakers had been set facing out to sea,
as is now pointed out by my parents shouting against the
noise, while we bite into *carpouzi*, watermelon, in despair, as
if the arc of glistening fruit and rind might act as a gag to

the distant DJ's choice. 'Take me to the station . . . put me on the train . . .'

For those of us of a generation to know the words, the agony may be worse or better—it's impossible to tell which—than that of my mother and father. It doesn't really matter anyway—the nights are ruined, and it's far too hot to close a window.

'We went to talk to the manager, and to the local police,' my father said.

'And,' my mother says, able to see the funny side even at this desperate time, 'we thought they were very polite and understanding.'

'The hotel changed the speakers around,' my father concurred. 'But then they returned to their original positions.'

'At least they didn't laugh when we were explaining it all to them,' puts in my mother. 'I mean, to them it must have sounded like those jokes about foreigners that the English make. "My husbang and I . . ." You know the sort of thing.'

Dinner over, we went indoors and then came out again, but nowhere was safe from the Stones. The music made the heat a hundred times more persistent, as if it had become tangible, an enemy. 'This is what I try to do,' my mother says when we finally go up to lie on our beds by the open window. She has shown us the tape recorder on the floor of her room; gone to close the three windows that open to the sea and the wood across the valley; and, despite the almost unbearable heat, she has trained herself to listen to tapes all night, to counteract the noise from the hotel.

The tapes play the sound of waves coming gently in on

a beach. We all laugh—and admire her ingenuity—but the nights, my mother says, are not uninterrupted after all. 'The machine clicks off, you see. And then, up until 2 a.m. or later, the imported ocean is replaced by the Stones.'

III

L es jours se suivent et se ressemblent tous.' This Racinian declaration, denoting an intolerable passage of time, can be translated into an expression of contentment at Rovinia. Days—and indeed years—have passed; and if they are not all exactly the same, they are alike enough to provide a sense of time passing as seen and felt in the antique world. Dominated by seasons, spring planting, late-summer harvests of olive and grape, and in months punctuated by celebrations and farewells, we come and go (though I more frequently than others) to this place that has mysteriously become home.

It's the late 1980s, and five years since my father died here, on 4th October 1983. He had suffered from the family heart disease (for which he'd undergone an operation seven years earlier, at the age of seventy-five) and had gone on with the rhythm of life at Rovinia as if nothing had happened. The sea and the bright sunlight continued to dominate his paintings; and the artist Ghika, coming to visit on a day when bay and point were swept by rain and lowering cloud, picked out a dark view of mountain and livid ocean as the best of the lot.

But it was Mathraki, the magical repository of fossils and flints, the low-lying island we visited in the big caique, with its health-infusing mud and white cluster of simple buildings, that my father most loved to paint. In those pale oils he did somehow capture the faintness of the blue in a sea that, unlike ours here on the deeply shelving west coast, lies shallow for miles, over sand; and the softly yellow promontory, crumbling down to its mirror image in the water below, is as much of an apparent illusion when approached in real life as in one of my father's many representations of Mathraki. At the time of his operation in London, the picture hung on the wall at the end of his bed. I saw him lie there and stare at it, as if the tubes that drained from his side and the rumble of traffic on a grey London day simply vanished in the presence of the island and its relics of a time that long pre-dated Odysseus's landing at the bay south of the palace of King Alcinous.

Because of the sense of one day blending into the next, here, there is also a strong sense of my father's continued occupation at Rovinia. The pride he took in the exactness of proportion comes back each time one steps out on to the terrace, or looks out through the width of the door into the room where he sat at the desk (another victim of the otherwise excellent Corfu carpenter, leading to squashed-knee syndrome) writing in longhand on the blue airmail pad that he and my mother bought at the stationer's before a quick drink at the Corfu Bar, and then home. The lightness of the house at every season of the year brings to mind his dislike—perhaps after a childhood in a fake Jacobean manor and then in an imitation Gothic castle—of the old, the dark, the fusty. Here, of course, my mother's own love of the 'nothing' of their bedroom, where the sea provides a violently blue and ever-changing wallpaper and there is otherwise on the walls only the whiteness of the light, joins my father's preference for the unpretentious and the plain.

I was in London with my two young daughters when news came of my father's last illness. It was quick—but there had been anguish; and the kindness and selflessness of the doctor and heart specialist, who came at night across an autumnal sea all the way from Paleocastritsa to our bay, was typical of the generosity of the Corfiot people. There was nothing, in fact, that could be done: my father, stretchered up the path by strong young men, spoke in a way that was as typical of him as the efforts by the doctor to help him had been of a Greek to a suffering stranger: this was the first time, the prone figure announced, that the landscape of groves and olives had been seen while lying supine. He declared his delight in seeing the land he had come to nearly twenty years before, from a stretcher—not many, my mother and I had to agree much later, would see their transportation to the clinic while seriously ill in quite this debonair and dispassionate light. Yet I understood, too, that this was not after all the very last journey for my father. His will stipulated that he be buried at Traquair in Scotland, and there, in a grave overlooking the hills of his youth, he was finally laid to rest. Marie Aspioti sent wild cyclamen, from the other hills he had come to love.

Since I'd been coming here, it had seemed to me that my parents grew younger and I—children, work, money all heavily engraved on my face and soul—had grown considerably older. The feeling of freedom enjoyed after a quarter of a century of office life was of course most evident in my father: but together, and with new friends (Michael and Mirabel Osler, who had been teachers in Asia and were now living in an old house beyond Gastouri on the cliffs overlooking the sea), he and my mother enjoyed trips and explorations on the island with the fervour of much younger people. The Greek sun, too, played its part: even in his eighties my father looked rakish and handsome in his straw hat, leading a middle-aged couple, siblings of an English writer friend, to mistake him on arrival by taxi-boat on our beach for—as my mother recounted—'a dashing beach bum in need of a tip'. ('But where,' said my father, on being told this intriguing compliment, 'where then *was* this tip?') His continuing presence, a reminder of his practical abilities, his humour and his love of a mystical past, lives on at Rovinia without any sense of a gloomy 'haunting'.

On this occasion, half a decade on from my father's death, we're on our way up to Liapades, to attend a christening. Yorgos of the Nikterida, the small taverna halfway down the steep hill on the outskirts of the village, has invited us to his house, not so far as the crow flies, but so

high in a narrow cobbled street above the houses and court-
yards shuttered and bolted against prying eyes that to arrive
there is to feel oneself permitted to enter the secret upper
floor of an intricate doll's house.

On the way there we pass the pretty church where it
seems only funerals take place—for all other functions are
presided over by the *papas* in the church in the main square.
This church, with its banana-yellow distempered walls and
picturesque cypresses, may make a picture suitable for a
tourist camera—but the cemetery, only half-screened from
the road by a low wall, is, quite literally, the last place anyone would want to be. There is clearly no tradition of seeing
to the upkeep of graves: weeds trail the chipped and
mildewed slabs of stone, which lean at perilous angles. It
would come as no surprise, when one hasty glance over the
wall is rewarded by the sight of oblong piles of earth long
neglected and refusing even a crop of grass to cover the
incumbent, to discover that corpses lay there, coffinless and
waiting for the next downpour, with the coming of the
autumn equinox, to wash away the thin counterpane of soil.
'Not here,' my mother says as we fall into the silence that
walking down the long stretch of road beside the cemetery
invariably produces. 'I did see that once—it wasn't here in
Liapades, but in Turkey. Dead people's toes were sticking up
out of the graves.'

We all fall into an even deeper silence, a picture of the
ancient Alexandros and his motionless white feet on our
beach below the house springing instantly to mind. Birth,
marriage and death are also never far from the surface in a
Greek community such as this; and we do not voice the

thought that today's celebration of a birth is an occasion we're grateful to be asked to join.

Not that a christening here can be expected to take place at all near the birth of the child. A good year or so can go by while the infant, still unnamed, grows into a lusty toddler— and I can't help admiring this slowness, similar to the long wait during betrothal for the day when a wedding can be planned, which appears to characterise Greek family life. After all, a couple can always decide *not* to marry, if they find each other's company uncongenial. And why does a child, unable to speak in its first year or so, actually need a name until fairly late on, if it comes to it?

The answer, as so often, turns out to be pragmatic. The infant, who must be plunged in cold water and be seen to be totally immersed, will not thrive if this rite is performed in the winter months. So a child born in spring must wait until the following spring or summer; and a winter birth will go a whole year and a half before the requisite conditions for baptism can be shown to exist. Today, a day when the sun seems set in the sky, fixed and without any intention of finding a cloud to obscure it, is clearly perfect for the christening of Yorgos's little granddaughter.

'What have you?' We remember the answers we were told, when we first came here, that are given to questions regarding the gender of a newborn. 'A son? *Tou Theou*' (from God). But if a daughter had been born, the hapless parent had but one answer: 'Excuse me!' We wonder if this remains the practice, in a community where, gradually, the modern world is being introduced. Do they say 'Excuse me' still, on the birth of a daughter? It seems unlikely, certainly, that the good-natured Yorgos will do anything other than welcome his female grandchild with open arms.

Of course I know the reasons here are pragmatic also. A daughter must provide a dowry: often, if a succession of bad harvests or misfortunes descends on the family, it is impossible to come up with the trees, the inch of land in the patchwork surrounding the village, the chest with its consignment of sheets and embroidered blankets. A daughter may not be able to afford to leave home and become the slave of another woman, her mother-in-law: she must upset the balance determined by nature and stay a slave at home. I think of the young Scottish—and English—girls who fall in love with the local lads out here, and goggle in amazement at what would have been expected of them, if they had been Greek. For they bring with them nothing at all; and are not loved by their elders here, for it.

Strips of intensely cultivated earth begin to appear, once we have left behind the misleadingly pretty yellow church and the cemetery. These are the allotments of the villagers: each strip no more than three or four feet wide and six feet long, as neat and well tended as the burial plots of similar dimensions are ignored. Onions grow here, the green fronds bright against the red-brown earth of the region. Carrots show feathery plumes. Spinach—essential for the popular and delicious dish *spanokopita*, the flaky pastry spinach tart served on special occasions—looks like a succession of dark bundles in the meticulously weeded ground. Soon, we think to ourselves as we trudge on, calves aching from the walk up from the house (and the fact that we've come on a road nearly all the way, albeit an unmade road, the all-important new way down to the sea at Yefira, doesn't prevent us from feeling that we're engaged in a marathon, if we're to climb all the way to the top of Liapades), soon we'll be enjoying the food and drink Yorgos and his wife will provide for the guests to the christening. 'Expect a lot of sugared almonds,' says my mother, who has participated in one of these events before. 'Very elaborate and expensive . . . dolls made of dragées, little tulle-covered baskets—and lots of lovely other things as well.'

While I'm thinking that there's something about these occasions, wherever they're celebrated, that demands identical fare to the year before—and the year before that, going back to the food prepared and ceremonially eaten by ya-ya and pro-ya-ya alike—I think also of the necessity of this sameness, to bring calm and reassurance to lives shaken by political change and frequent economic disaster. Liapades had been known as one of the 'Red' villages of the area, at the time of the Civil War that succeeded the Second World War. Communists and their foes fought and died here, within living memory—indeed, within the lifespan of people who still aren't enormously old. Then, the military junta had placed its iron fist over these lives. Only the poet George Seferis had the courage to speak out against the regime—he was the first of many intellectuals exiled by the colonels' seizing of power in Greece. Seferis, Ambassador in London, issued a statement that included the warning that 'a regime has been imposed on us which is totally inimical to the ideals for which our world—and our people so resplendently—fought during the last world war . . .' For this—and for his assertion that 'in the case of dictatorial regimes the beginning may seem easy, but tragedy awaits, inevitably, in the end. The drama of this ending haunts us consciously and unconsciously—as in the immemorial choruses of Aeschylus'—Seferis had his diplomatic passport revoked.

What did the relatives and friends of the people of Liapades, those who climb ahead of us now up the steep main street, make of the regime, now in turn overthrown, with its tyranny and constrictions?

We are *xenoi*, foreigners who never can really know. But we are invited to partake in a ceremony and feast that have outlived the recent political change and upheaval. Yorgos will have lit his fires in the Nikterida charcoal grill and he'll bring up to his house *cocoretsi*—the speciality some find hard to stomach (because it is indeed made of stomach, a sheep's offal stuffed in a long stocking of fat, not unlike the Scottish haggis). There will be chicken; the ubiquitous and ever-desirable *xoriatiki* salad; and feta that is firm, moist and just right for eating. Then will come the bright, sweet-pea-coloured sugared almonds, traditional fare for a christening.

The courtyard with its lemon and orange trees in their white knee-socks—the trunks of the trees slender, and a bright array of marigolds and geraniums like flowers painted in a frieze around their base—is already crowded with relatives and guests. Aunts, grandmothers, cousins and second cousins throng the yard and climb the wooden stairs to the main rooms, as Yorgos comes beaming towards us, hand outstretched. He does his best to introduce us and explain the patchwork, here at its most intensely interwoven (though there are clans, obviously, in Liapades, who have no kin with his family at all) and we listen as he indicates sisters, nieces and a posse of very young children who will, he says with a secret grin of satisfaction, be amongst those to run out in the street and hear the child's name when it is proclaimed.

We go up the outside stairs, to find that the ceremony will shortly begin. A sudden hospitable rush: Yorgos, who makes the Nikterida restaurant, despite its site on one of the steepest hairpin bends in the locality, the most agreeable place in Liapades to sit and enjoy a meal, sees us in his home and without seats or drinks, and bustles to provide both. He remembers ouzo for my mother and myself, and beer for Tim, my partner of a few years now and as passionately interested in Rovinia and the surrounding countryside and legends as we are. How fortunate we are, I think as the inevitable shared glass of water is proffered, a drop from this turning the aniseed drink as white and cloudy as just-mixed distemper; how delicious Yorgos's olives, black and larger than ours, and with the true taste of Greece: bitter, life-giving, older even than the wine Dionysus quaffs in the bas-relief in the little museum in the town.

But just as we acclimatise to the noise up here—to the old women who shriek greetings to each other from room to room; to the young boys who run, in a desperate effort to amuse themselves, between the legs of the guests and under the table where the food is laid out—a silence falls as loud and excited as the din. The *papas* walks into the room. He's tall, bearded (as the Orthodox priest must be) and has a kindly face: my mother whispers that she had known him when she first came to live at Rovinia, when he was still a boy. He precedes what appears at first to be a large bucket, filled with water; but, as it comes closer, this can be seen to be a kind of primitive urn, deep and containing the holy element right up to the brim. No wonder, I think, it has to be sunny weather for a small child to be subjected to total immersion in this: it might be as well, too, if the candidate for baptism could already swim.

We've come to know the baby on our visits to Nikterida. Under the trellis with the vine that grows as sparse as balding hair, if you sit too far along the small terrace by the side of the road, she lies in her pram oblivious to the churn of lorries or the clip-clop of donkeys and mules as they head up the shortcut into the main street of Liapades. We've had her held up to us for inspection and seen her smile—and each time we've neglected to remember that she has no name. 'Beba,' says her grandmother, when we search for it; she is a handsome dark-haired woman who works in the kitchen with Yorgos, producing the *calamaraki*, squid in a light batter with lemon—which we come up the path to eat, rain or shine. 'Beba.' And we're reminded of the fact that the all-important christening has not yet taken place.

By the time the baby has had the shock of being plunged into the water—and has begun to scream, accordingly—the chatter and yell of the party have started up again. In church, the *papas* is accustomed to calling for quiet (he is always unsuccessful), so loud are the chatting, commenting voices of the congregation. Here, that moment of silence at his appearance is all God is likely to get.

Still, we're close enough to the action to be able to hear the *papas* as he speaks his (alas, incomprehensible to us) litany over the infuriated and violently shivering child. The scene, in the main front room of the house—this room one storey above ground, to give space to animals and stored hay and foodstuffs below—is one that could have taken place at any time in the past five hundred years or so. The priest, in the gloomy shade of the low room; the baby, its flesh tones vivid after the inundation in water; the proud faces of Yorgos and his wife and their daughter Marina, the baby's mother, caught in the strong beam of sunlight that comes straight into the middle of the scene—these could comprise a painting or sketch by a provincial artist, executed in the eighteenth or nineteenth century.

Now comes another kind of sound; and this time a real silence appears like a gaping hole around it. 'ATHINA,' is shouted loudly from the wooden walkway that runs along the first floor of the house, out into the street. 'ATHINA!'

So, the baby is named. The outside world has been told that Yorgos's granddaughter is Athina. And the *koumbari*, godparents, who have chosen it are joined by all the rest of the guests, everyone throwing coins down to the posse of young boys, now beyond the gates of the house and standing, palms high above their heads to catch the money, in the street.

The sugared almonds, some elaborately contrived as horses, carriages, dolls in crinolines, come round. As we crack the hard white sugar covering and crunch into the nut beneath, Yorgos comes running up. Wine flows—he tries to explain more to us—but the chattering and laughing and kissing and back-thumping are fully under way again. It's late, and the sun much lower in the sky, when we make our way down the road to Yefira and then across the terraces of olives and fig and orange trees to Rovinia.

Now that the village has water, electricity and TV, stories of only a few years back seem to belong to a medieval world. Angeliki, she who was punished just after the war for permitting herself to be seduced by an Italian and was thrust down on a brazier of burning coals by her father—what happened to her, what was her story? The secretive, Moorish atmosphere of Liapades makes one want to know the outcome of this brutal treatment: did Angeliki marry, was she able finally to make a life for herself? Or was she kept cloistered at home—maybe even put with nuns to live out her days?

I'm given some, but not all, of the answers as we stand in what must be the place with one of the most beautiful views in the Mediterranean. The monastery above Paleocastritsa—Theotockou monastery, as it is called—stands on a hill that looks almost manufactured, with its perfect rotundity and sheer steepness: a breast, emerging suddenly from the silver-green of olive-wooded Paleocastritsa, and the church with its dome a nipple on the peak. The bell-tower is probably the most photographed of its kind in all the Greek islands.

To enter the monastery is to combine old and new worlds. Arched and whitewashed walls, paraded by the odd monk in long black robe against the dazzle of the annually renewed whiteness, belong to the timelessness portrayed in postcard and guide book. The little shop, selling icons and other religious items, is glossy and expensive. And the interior of the church, for all the gloom, lit tapers and handsome iconostasis, has long ago lost the sense and atmosphere of reverence and worship. Wide doors are kept open, on the side that faces the magnificent view. A small garden, as well kept as a child's garden with its rows of daisies, red lobelias and box hedges so trim no-one would dare interfere with the flowerbeds within, is set under prunus trees before a low wall—and the long drop to the unending, glorious blue. The monastery is one of the first ports of call—after the souvenir and sheepskin-rug stalls that straggle at the foot of the hill—of the world's tourists. It remains pretty; and some of the peace that must once have reigned here can still, especially before the season begins, be found there. The tourists, when they disembark from the buses and coaches and hired cars and mopeds, are stopped at the gate and handed clothes to cover their nudity: skirts for the women, jackets for the men.

'She was here until a short time ago,' says Helena, a woman who knows the history and secrets of most village's and big families in Corfu. 'But I don't see her today—a little old woman with specs, she hands out the skirts to the women tourists, which they must wear to go into the monastery.'

'Who? Angeliki?' we all ask. It seems fitting that a daughter treated so badly by her father should be cared for in this place, where everything resembles the colours of an icon of the forgiving Madonna: gold and white and blue.

'No,' we are told. 'Not Angeliki. She married, soon after her punishment for losing her virginity to an Italian. The man she married had property by the sea.'

We all go to the low wall and look out at the coast that stretches south from Paleocastritsa and disappears into a haze of blue. There is our beach, with the house at Rovinia no bigger than a thumbnail; on one of the neighbouring beaches down by the shoreline Angeliki must have lived, happy at last, we hope, with a man who has forgotten her past disgrace.

'Angeliki was childless,' Helena goes on. 'And her husband wanted children. So he went up to the village with a nice big fish, and asked a young girl he found there to come to his house and live with him and his wife.'

'That can't have worked out very well,' someone says.

'Indeed it did not. The husband seduced the poor girl. She did give birth to a child, but it died.'

'And then?' Suddenly the beauty of the place where we stand, the neat garden divided into triangles and rectangles of bright flowers, and the stunning view all the way down to the shipwreck of Odysseus's boat, gives little but a headache. We watch a group of Scandinavian tourists, red with sunburn in their Paisley-print borrowed skirts, as they push their way into the interior of the church.

'They turfed the poor girl out. But her father wouldn't take her back. He did worse by her than that—this is a story like *The Scarlet Letter*, I'm afraid to say. He made her walk round the village with a banner; pinned to it was money and written on the banner were the words "This Is the Price of My Dishonour".'

We don't ask what happened next. The fathers of the village rise in our minds and we choke on indignation. Was all this so long ago, after all?

'She's the one with rimless spectacles who gives out the skirts here to the tourists,' our friend tells us. 'The monastery took her in, you see. But she doesn't seem to be here today. Poor old girl,' she ends absently.

We'd seen Costa a couple of times. He was the sharp-looking one, from a village about twelve miles distant: his hair was the dyed blond-with-black-roots variety that denotes the entrepreneur, the wide-boy, in this neck of the woods; and his jacket was black leather, his wristwatch huge and spiked like the wheel of a motorbike.

Today we're on a trip to some of the nearby villages, taking the back roads Tim walks with such delight and vigour; and it so happens that we walk into a grocery shop/*cafeneon* and see at once the difference in this venue from the sleepy little stores we've grown used to nearer home. For this shop appears to have decided to give up being a shop altogether. The odd plastic bucket hangs from the ceiling, still there due to the indifference and laziness of the owner, rather than an indication of actually being for sale; and a few shelves that had once been stacked with cans of food, shiny blue school notebooks faded by the sun and the bars of chocolate and packets of cigarettes so essential to the fortunes of a Greek retailer, contain only a trace of their former wares.

The rest of the shop has been turned, quite simply, into a gambling den. A table with a green baize cloth takes up the space at the back, with the hanging, shaded light reminiscent of an American *film noir*; and a bar runs along where once the old wooden counter would almost certainly have been. One or two men, heavily stubbled and acting the parts expected of gamblers, sit already on the rickety wooden chairs provided—these being the sole reminder of the old, innocent days when a *metriou* or *vari gliko*, Turkish coffee medium or very sweet, was served along with ouzo and a lump of *loukoumi*, the Turkish delight so pale and smothered in fine sugar that its colour and flavour can barely be discerned. As we walk in, feeling ourselves already unwanted in this surprising new setting, three other men push past us and go to the green baize table. One of them we recognise from Alipa Bay, where the big caique is moored: he is Stefanos, a fisherman who comes with his taxi-boat to Rovinia Beach in high season and deposits tourists below our house for the day.

Stefanos has a carrier bag with him. We begin to offer a greeting—for on occasions Stefanos has come up the steps and offered lobster or *sinegrida* or *barbouni*, the red mullet that grows rarer in this sea each year. He is seldom negotiated with—for his prices are astronomical, and we know the hotels are expected to pay less than we are asked. Nevertheless, we do know him; and as it's evident he has a new catch in the carrier bag, we look at it with the interest that a potential buyer is expected to show.

As it turns out, the last thing Stefanos wants is a buyer for his exciting new catch. He fails to meet the eye of any one of us; and if we hadn't felt something quite interesting was just about to take place, in this modest grocery store across the narrow village street from another such—the one opposite, however, the traditional type, with old men in flat caps sitting outside and black-clad women by the counter with its weighing machine, picking out food and ancient vegetables in the dark interior—we would have turned and crossed the few feet of cobbles to normality.

We are right to wait, though the scowls that come in our direction are not what we are accustomed to, in this most courteous country. Having learnt early on in travels through northern Greece and the Peloponnese that the apparent surliness of the country folk is due to the fact that they must be greeted before they will return a greeting—this discovery bring us much relief here, for the angry, shut-in expression on the face of a man or woman encountered when walking will turn to a radiant smile and a series of '*Heretes*' followed by a string of personal questions, once the greeting has been proclaimed—we are surprised by the lack of response on the part of the gamblers at the green baize table.

The reluctance to have us included in the company is explained when Costa enters the shop-cum-bar. Without looking to right or left, and in sunglasses of a size and black-ness that would suggest he entirely fails to see our little party by the entrance, the organiser of the den—as he patently is—strides over to Stefanos and takes the carrier bag from him.

Cards spring into spirals and arches as shuffling rapidly takes place and Costa is handed a wad of notes by each player. The game begins. None of us can see accurately what it is; but soon enough, throwing down their cards, players are disqualified from participating. More cigarettes are lit as the losers gather by the bar. Metaxas, the Greek brandy loved by everyone here (though whisky, considered more of a snob's drink, is gaining popularity) is poured into glasses. Everyone watches as the contest narrows to two men.

It's at this point that we notice that the back pocket of Costa's jeans is bulging with drachmas. And it's then we begin to understand the nature of the 'Fish Auction' he masterminds. For the winner—now the game has ended and a young man in a frayed jacket and with a satisfied expression has thrown down the winning hand—is handed his prize by Costa. He has won the carrier bag of Stefanos's catch of fish.

'Of course, Costa bought the fish from Stefanos,' we say when we're safely in a village nearer home, and sitting in the back yard of a store—a back yard in Lakones, which has a sensational view of sea, mountains and petrified boat. 'Then he goes on to make a good profit by charging the players a fee to join the game.'

'And the winner,' someone points out, 'may have won a great big fish, which he can sell for a profit down at the hotel in Paleocastritsa.'

'Or,' someone else chips in, 'he can find he's landed with a load of little fish that have no value at all.'

'Then they'll go in his brother-in-law's freezer,' we say together, picturing the motorbike as it goes up the vertiginous streets of a mountain village, the load tied to the back emptied into the deep-freeze in the kitchen of a house shuttered against the afternoon sun.

We also think of Costa and his black leather jacket, and the bulging jeans with their growing load of drachmas.

We've brought our picnic, to enjoy in this most secret, modest and beautiful spot. The shop, which fronts on the street in Lakones, supplies us with ouzo; water so fresh and cold it must have been drawn from a spring in Athene's grove, which leads down to the sea; and beer. The retsina, Kourtaki, comes in bottles with tops that are prised off with a bottle-opener. We have boiled eggs, Maria's *tarama* with bread, and olives from Rovinia, small and delicious. The sun is strong, and we sit away from the railing that sticks out over the great chasm, enjoying the small amount of shade we can find. The shop owner brings us tiny cups of china so thick and white there is barely any room for the *metriou* inside. We leave, after I've succumbed, as I so often do, to the 'need' for another of the blue school notebooks in which I write. The gambling den seems to belong to another world as we stand by the till in the deep gloom of the shop, salami and shears and nylon gloves hanging in a thicket above our heads.

Inflation haunted Greece in the 1970s and 1980s and my father would sit worrying over his accounts in the little study off the main living room. Everything now cost a fortune, and he was glad to have built a studio at the back of the house in time to avoid the worst ravages. When in there, he was happy—and producing increasingly professional landscapes of village streets where sheep walk down between houses heavy with the strong-smelling mauve wisteria; and of meadows with the olive trees he had come to love, standing guard over a carpet of wild flowers.

We would go into the town, but often returned for our midday meal, arriving after a morning's excitement hungry, thirsty and hot. We knew that to jump into the sea was to lose the memory almost instantly of the long queue to park in the wide grounds of the Esplanade, and the sometimes perilous drive home, with roads that have sheer drops into unfenced drains, and brown-and-white Corfiot dogs, angry and demented by the long hours they spend chained up, on occasions breaking free and running under our wheels. The sea is the great cleanser, of body and soul: to feel at first that you are entering the heart of a sapphire or an aquamarine, then to sink deeper into water that has cold springs as refreshing as a subaqueous shower, is to know that you will come out transformed, like a creature in Ovid's *Metamorphoses*, and begin the day again as if you had gone nowhere at all.

Not that going into town is anything but a pleasurable experience. In April and May the cherry and Judas trees around the vast Esplanade are as pink and magenta and red as paper streamers, tossing in the wind. Carriages with horses make the necessary tourist picture—but are actually a good way to get about, as the cars with their chain-smoking, impatient drivers can cause long waits and snarled-up routes. And the tall Venetian buildings, many in streets so narrow they are hard to appreciate, the balconies swathed in washing, and the shutters and grilles and pots of geraniums with the obligatory island cats, give a stifling sense of a way of life that most certainly has not changed since the seventeenth or eighteenth century.

The town's freshness is provided by the shops that spill out their fruit and leaves on to the pavement. 'Let's have *carpouzi*,' my daughter says with longing, as the great dark-green watermelons, with their ruby interiors and pips as fierce as rows of ebony teeth, are pulled from the stall and weighed and jiggled in the hand. In the market, where strange new fads arrive with every changing scene in world affairs, my mother snaffles a blue-glass sugar bowl from Russia, just after that country opens up to the West. There are lacy pillowcases as well as tiny fish, lights of old Venetian glass and bundles of asparagus, all together.

Corfu town is famed for its jewellery, and there are so many shops flashing gold, gold against peach velvet cushions, gold in dark-blue enamel surrounds, gold ugly and (sometimes) old and beautiful. Rings tempt young girls: tourmaline and chrysoprase green as the sea we have left on the other side of the island; rings of dark cornelian set in silver, which are pulled out in trays by chuckling old men. But we must take care over money, and we head instead to the Corfu Bar for cappuccino and Campari and the buzz that comes from sitting in the arcade and being one of the crowd. Newspapers, gossip—the chatter, the long-drawn-out syllables of Corfiot talk that is like the swallows' incessant converse at home, bring us into the world, we who are often weeks on end only with each other and the sea for company.

The Corfu Bar makes a mockery of any budget; but it's agreed that a coffee there, frothy and white-topped, is worth the price. Besides, the Listón, as this imitation of the rue de Rivoli in Paris is known, is an arcade of many cafés; it borders on the Esplanade and is fringed by trees that give shade to the strolling shoppers beneath. As it grows dark, the 'real' inhabitants come out to walk up and down; but we are seldom there then, unless we've had to go into the town in the late afternoon for some appointment or other. Evening is succeeded by night quickly here, and to stumble across the terraces from the Yefira road with bags of shopping in the dark is not easy, even if we've remembered our torches. The town is for the day; and what we bring back with us needs the yellow, affirming sun to show the desirability of our purchases. For we have nearly always, despite window-shopping in the market and main shopping street, returned with the Greek powder paint we love to put on the walls back in a cold northern country; and also with the striped cotton, generic to this island, which is good for curtains and for fixing on battens on the walls.

The powder paint has as its most irresistible colour a strong, bright blue, the blue of lapis lazuli and of the simplest Greek houses, which are oases of blue, either plain or diluted with whitewash, all over Corfu. This is the blue we imagine will transform our lives away from the sun; but alas, it grows dark and sullen in grey climates and needs to be mixed with white and dragged across the walls, to prevent it becoming oppressive.

As for the thin cotton, with its slightly seersucker appearance, wrinkled and transparent, this often proves an even greater disaster when it leaves here for cooler shores. The rooms in the Wing have the red-and-white variety of the cotton fixed to the walls and used as curtains in all the rooms—but in London this looks cheap and see-through, its magic evaporating completely without the backing of the sun. The cotton also comes in green-and-white—'how fresh!' visitors exclaim when standing over the bales in the shop in the old Jewish quarter in the town. Rafael, the shop owner, was one of the few Jews to return to Corfu after the mass deportation by the Germans in 1943, and he smiles with delight as he spreads the green-and-white, the red-and-white and the blue-and-white stripes in a medley of peppermint candy colours across the counter. Our friends buy, dreaming already of their wonderfully altered flats where the Greek sun has come back in their suitcase, along with the blue—or deep red, or ochre—powder paint they have found in great sacks in the ironmonger's shop where we go to buy it, near the market. Never, we agree as we unload our buys on reaching the terrace at Rovinia and the enticing rush down to the pebble beach, does the sun seem so far away as when we take these simple acquisitions home.

When in Corfu, we aren't always understood by the Corfiots. We pull our cotton striped bedlinen out of its brown-paper wrapping and show it to Maria, who agrees that it is *poli oreia* (very beautiful), but at heart, I suspect, thinks we are crazy to want to put it on walls or use it for curtains with rough wooden poles and big wooden hoops that frequently split apart like deranged earrings. We open the little packages of paint and stare into the heart of blue—the blue, as Lawrence Durrell says, that is like the blue of the sea that changes as you cross the Ionian Sea from Calabria. How can this blue, identified as the true blue of Greece, fail you when it gets home? Thus, along with the craze for olive oil and sun-dried tomatoes, do the northerners act out their fantasies of a Mediterranean life at home.

It's a bright, warm day in early May and we're sitting on the small terrace of the Nikterida, at a long table with friends from the other side of the island, on the second Sunday after Easter, the festival of the *Mille Fiori*. Clearly by origin a Venetian festival to celebrate the great burst of life that comes in May to every field and forest, what we see now couldn't be more Greek. A procession winds down the road from the church in Liapades' main square, carrying banners and a great portrait of Jesus Christ that normally hangs in the church; everyone is in uniform; and the noise from the brass band is deafening.

I wonder aloud what happened to Dassia, whose betrothal party we attended all those years ago in the house she would shortly exchange for her parents-in-laws' home, up the street in Liapades. She'd wanted to play the trumpet in the brass band.

'Dassia,' says a Liapades dweller who has overheard, and who pauses to lean across our table, already bedecked with Yorgos's olives ('Hmm,' says Maria, 'not as good as ours at Rovinia') and ouzo in tall glasses, with Kourtaki retsina glinting yellow on the table. 'Dassia was not popular with her fiancé for this decision. He did not wish her to be in the band.'

'So what happened?' we ask, all hoping against hope that some fierce punishment had not been meted out to the girl for voicing this unusual demand.

'She told him she will choose the band,' replies our informant, before stepping down the few steps into the street, and almost straight into the array of dark uniformed legs and brass instruments. He is swallowed up by the sound and ferocious marching, and disappears from sight.

By the time we've scanned the players of trumpet, bassoon and drum, the procession has rounded the corner and gone on down the road, past the school playground with its assortment of swings and slides, looking out over a breath-taking view of our own mountains, and the newly green village allotments lying on the extremity of the plain beneath the great blue-grey shadows of the range.

With the march-past now safely out of sight—even Christ's wispy hair and halo in the giant portrait are no longer visible after the bend in the road has been navigated—the traffic that has been held up all morning comes down from the heights of Liapades with a vengeance. White vans, carrying perhaps more provisions for the feast at Agios Thodoros, the tiny church two miles to the east; cars hooting joyously, as if it's a wedding that is being celebrated, not a religious festival; donkeys (but far fewer than there were in the early days here) with their ancient riders, faces brown and wrinkled as they peer up at the newly powerful sun.

And girls, girls on mopeds and driving small cars; girls in jeans and some in frayed denim shorts, cut off at the knee; girls in traditional (and by now this means the Fifties, not the tourist 'peasant costume') swirly dresses and cardigans discreetly buttoned at the waist. But, inevitably, it's the girls on mopeds—so independent, so many aeons of time away from the hapless Angeliki or her successor, the wearer of the Scarlet Letter in Liapades—who grab my attention. The women in black gathering firewood on their beasts could be the mothers and aunts of these bike-riders; in reality they appear to be no relation at all. Dassia, it seemed, had been one of the first to express her own desires, when she chose membership of the brass band over a husband who wished to deny her the pleasure of exercising her musical gifts. I can't help wondering, all the same, whether the linen and embroidered blankets had to be carried back down the street again when she announced her decision.

We've just come from the fair at Agios Thodoros. Stalls were laid out under the olive trees, great rafts of plastic toys with small children goggling round them; bales of shiny material; and cups and saucers and vases and glass of every description. At a table in the shade was a posse of *papases* (if this is the right collective noun) and their wives, sipping ouzo and trying the fearsomely sweet *baklava*, the honey-and-filo-pastry tooth-stinger that is a reminder of Middle Eastern taste and its lasting influence, even as far west as this former colony of Venice and France. My mother went to sit with them a while; and says now, as we reminisce about the people we saw at the *Mille Fiori*, that she had known most of the grey- and white-bearded priests when they were young boys earning pocket money waiting at table at the Tourist Pavilion in Paleocastritsa. 'And Achilleos,' I say, for I had recognised the man, now old and frail, who had dug unsuccessfully for a well at Rovinia before the miraculous coming of Colonel Merrilees. 'And Thekli,' someone else says—she one of the women who had borne cement and bricks and stone in baskets on her head up the newly carved-out steps to Rovinia House from the beach. As we remember the days of building, we also know those days will never return—and a very good thing too, for the women, though the men who sit in cafés or out in village streets by the open doors of grocery shops, playing *tavli* or simply staring into space, show no sign of taking their place in agricultural or construction work.

The religious nature of the day has my mother and her

friends from an old house south of Corfu town (Neil and Marilli McVicar they are called, he a retired Edinburgh judge, she from the Corfiot family who had previously owned the relic of St Spiridon, the Vulgaris) talking of miracles and hauntings and the like. We all know the story of the haunted house at Koundara, an eighteenth-century stone house between Liapades and Corfu town; indeed, we have all been there. But the necessary chill on a day of feasting—the ghost story in the machine—demands a repetition of the strange saga of a house cursed with ill-fortune.

More than two hundred years ago the son of the rich Cretan owner of Koundara, an imposing house on a hill, which boasts a beautiful Venetian well, became ill with fever. He was the adored eldest son and the Cretan made haste to go and pray to St Spiridon to save him.

So the story begins. We wait, like waiting for the guillotine blade to come whistling down, for the next instalment.

'The son died,' says one of the appointed storytellers. 'And the father proceeded to curse the saint.'

'Then followed a chapter of disasters,' puts in the next teller of the tale. 'The house changed hands several times.'

'Ill-luck befell every owner. Most died in their prime after they had owned the house for a short time. Local people still report accidents and illnesses with their livestock.'

It's true—though I'm reluctant to believe these tales of curses and magic here. There are so many of these; even the most respectable and pragmatic of senior citizens in a neighbouring village has recently reported the sight of his neighbour, an equally respectable village dweller, flying on a broomstick over his roof. Koundara does sound a bad investment, however, psychologically at least—though the latest account of the happenings surrounding the fate of the new owner, a rich Australian, are more easily to be believed.

'The well at Koundara,' the story starts up again, 'was made inaccessible to the local people by the new owner. He put a fence across the path they had always used to get water for themselves and their animals. So, one day, when the owner went down to the well, he got an unpleasant surprise. The well was blocked up. Someone—and possibly it was not St Spiridon—had filled it right up with cement.'

Yorgos has *arni* (lamb) today on the spit over the charcoal—as he does at Easter and often on a Sunday. The burnt, sizzling pieces of meat arrive; and, for some of us, the *calamaraki* in batter that we like above all else here. Athina—she whose christening we witnessed all those years ago—cuts neat strips of carrot and tomato and shreds lettuce, to make our salad; *tsatsiki* is delicious here, the cucumber fresh and the *yaourti* quite unlike the contents of mass-produced cartons in supermarkets at home. As we eat, red wine comes to accompany the meat—and more of the humble but excellent Kourtaki is brought to the table. Spirits rise: the sad story of the haunted house at Koundara fades like a phantom at dawn, even in the most recent tale of yet another owner finding his famous library destroyed there, from rain coming in through the roof. No—this is the time for the retelling of our own miracle: the miracle of the small caique and its disappearance at sea.

Eleni, Yorgos's wife, brings the complimentary glass of Metaxas cognac after the meal—but we are all by now drunk on the story of the big caique, the *Falaina*, whose length is twelve yards and whose width four yards, as she sets out to the island of Othono, about thirty miles west of Corfu, with my parents and a handful of friends on board. The size and solid nature of the big caique saved her on that dreadful day; but the little *Falaina*, towed in her wake, was not so fortunate.

The storm had been very quick to get up—quicker than my father had ever known in his years at sea. They'd all had a perfect day, swimming in clear water and resting in the shade provided by trees on the edge of the water. They'd discussed going on to Diabolos, the island called after the Devil—the Double, by reason of its being split in exactly two halves—and a repository, for pebble and stone collectors, of amazing red, green and ochre stones, good to place in dishes on tables around the house.

It was a day of a soft blueness, the sea stretching out under the overhead light of the sun. What could go wrong—when the barometer in the hall at Rovinia, consulted every five minutes before departure, had its needle comfortably positioned between CHANGE and FAIR, a position it had enjoyed for the past week?

The answer was sudden and terrifying. No sooner had the bathing party got under way in the big *Falaina*—the little *Falaina*, as ever, securely tied to the stern of the caique, with Thodoros's shoes still on the white-painted seat that runs along both sides of the craft—than all hell broke loose. It was, the passengers, reported, as if a B-movie with especially terrible special effects had been put on a great screen in the sky: the difference was that you weren't a spectator, but a participant. A violent gale got up. The sea roared and rose high over the deck of the big *Falaina*. Everyone huddled down in the cabin, though it was hard enough to get down the ladder steps to it; only my father, remaining on deck, saw that the little *Falaina*'s rope had broken and the small caique had gone bobbing off by itself.

Scrambling halfway up the galley steps, the passengers on the big *Falaina* saw the little boat recede into the distance, and then become obscured by rain and the black mist that seemed to permeate everything. This was goodbye to the little *Falaina*. She would never be seen again.

The succeeding days—when Rovinia had safely been reached and the bad news broken to Yorgos and Yannis and others pulling their boats, in this unprecedentedly bad weather, right up into the grove for safety—were ones of muted spirits and dejection. St Spiridon was prayed to, up in the church at Liapades. The statuette of the saint, given to my mother by Steven Runciman (not a close friend, but a Corfu-lover), was applied to frequently, on its table by the end of the white sofa in the living room. But everyone knew there could be no hope for a small caique in conditions such as these. The terrible wind that had taken it was a *maestro*, the wind from the north-west, so the boat must have blown miles south by now, perhaps even to the shores of Africa— or, more probably, had been wrecked against the rocks and cliffs of the southern part of the island.

Thodoros was driving to Paleocastritsa when he passed the only gap on the road from which Rovinia Beach can be seen, and what he saw caused him to stamp on the brakes. On the by-now calm blue sea, what was unmistakably the small *Falaina* was making her way towards Rovinia Bay.

'I had said that morning, which was five days after we lost the boat,' my mother recalls, 'wouldn't it be wonderful if the boat came bobbing in today?'—to which, as she remembers, my father had replied that this was pure fantasy.

'And it did,' my mother says. 'Thodoros drove at break-neck speed down to Alipa Bay, jumped on one of the fishing-boats and went at full throttle after the *Falaina*. He jumped boats and boarded her in mid-bay, leaving the astonished fishermen to turn and go back to Alipa. The little *Falaina* was perfectly safe and dry, after five days of the appalling storm. The *maestro* had changed to an easterly wind and blown her north again, so we must suppose. But she was only a few hundred yards from Rovinia when Thodoros caught her: of all the bays on the coast, this was the place she was coming home to, Thodoros's shoes still safely on the seat in the stern.'

This miracle, she added, had put up the stock of Rovinia in the village considerably at the time.

A family of stilts has come to visit our beach. Long scarlet legs of an impossible thinness support small, round bodies with black wings and white markings; the red beak, as much of a caricature as the wading legs, is long and curved.

It's autumn and we're beginning to feel it. Now the stilts, which we watch from the foot of the steps, stalk elegantly in the shallows just a few feet below the spot where old Alexandros, the crazy man of Liapades, liked to lie in the hot spring sun (too many tourists frightened him off when the season got under way). We imagine these birds, summer visitors, are pausing here before flying south; for the moment, it seems, they are happy on this shore, despite its sudden shelving to deep water. They've flown up from the lagoon, most probably—where we go to picnic by the long stretches of flat seawater, finding a tree to sit under and sometimes clumps of pink lilies growing wild in the sand. Stilts like saltpans and shallow water: they'll be off soon, dipping one last time into the lagoon before making the long journey back to winter sun.

Although the sea is still a wonderful seventy-six degrees Fahrenheit, we are aware of the slight chill in the evenings and come out on the terrace with a shawl. It grows dark earlier; so we peer in gloom at the pots of curly-leafed basil that we want to pick for tonight's pesto sauce with the spaghetti. The little glass jugs for wild flowers are getting filled as frequently as in the spring, and we go into the downstairs cloakroom to fill them with water we now take for granted, water from the mains that supplies the whole village (but this has been the case for many years)—and now also Rovinia.

The new spring brought by the coming of autumn is one of the glories of Corfu. Wild cyclamen, tentative at first, the pale-purplish stems seeming too fragile and naked to survive, are in fact long-flowering and hardy; the leaves, when they join them, have exquisite patterns of darkest green and silver. The autumn crocus, the same colour as the cyclamen, is actually frail; the patch here, down by oleander bushes that have grown enormous in the past few years, must be searched for carefully in long grass brought by the season's first downpour of rain.

A strong yellow flower, which appears at first to be the crocus of April and May, is in fact sternbergia, with egg-bright blooms that cheer the walk up the stone steps from the sea, when a *maestro* is blowing. It really is a rebirth here, of every kind of flower—tiny white narcissi appear near the autumn crocus and dwindle to nothingness in a matter of days; snowdrops have shown themselves in the long crumbling terraces at the back of the garden. As we approach winter, we are in spring.

Maria can be seen down in the grove, stooping by the roots of the olive trees, and we go down to join her. It's not olive-picking she's engaged in—the olives in this new age drop on to great black nylon nets, which have been laid down some time ago to catch them. No, Maria has seen mushrooms; and we poke about on the slopes up near the bridge over the riverbed, seeking chanterelles with their foxy hue.

Even the sea wears an autumn coat today, the last day of October and my final day here this year. A mush of discarded olive skins—its name, appropriately, is *mourga* in Greek—has been tipped into the sea further up the coast and spreads its deep stain over the pale water. We swim round it, feeling when the wind gets up and the waves bring it over to us the oily bath that the bay at Rovinia has suddenly become.

The road down to Yefira from the turning up to Liapades would not be recognised by anyone who had failed to come here over the past ten years. It is lined with low-level supermarkets and red-and-white villas—these advertise 'Rooms' for tourists fortunate enough to find this spot—and each has a huge swimming pool, spotlessly clean and a wonderful artificial blue under the olive trees. Yefira Bay has two large hotels now, The Cricketers and Eli Beach; and, as counterpoint to the new marble floors and 'American' bars, a sign is to be seen on the hotel noticeboard announcing that donkey rides up to the village can be arranged through Adonis. His house can be glimpsed through the trees; already a queue has formed in the foyer of The Cricketers for this brief and characterless excursion.

There is no electricity down at sea level at Rovinia, this in order to discourage a sudden sprouting of hotdog stalls on the beach. The tourists' appetite for hot snacks is catered for instead by a rowing-boat with a thatched roof, and from this ark toasted sandwiches and Coke are dispensed by a nephew of Maria's. When the laziness—or meanness—of the tourists at Rovinia becomes evident, the ark sails serenely south, to catch the hordes who go down the coast on the big tourist caiques from Paleocastritsa.

Rovinia is changed, but it remains much the same. In spring asphodels poke up in the long strip of land next to the riverbed; in autumn we pick our way past squills, tall and white as ghost lupins on the stony ground. There is a new hotel right across the bay, next to the Akrotiri, which nearly drove everyone to distraction with its disco music that boomed across the water. But years ago the music stopped coming; and the nights, with the piping from the scops owl (or tree frog) in the wood opposite is just as it was when the house first went up here.

'Kala ximona'—have a good winter—is what they say in the tavernas and gift shops on the road to Yefira when to saison has ended. On his walks Tim will not find espadrilles in a hidden shop, to bring back for us; a beer is even harder to find, with cafés shutting up and owners and workers going hard for harvesting the olives. Paths will be blocked off, so that the casual walker can't trample the black, bitter livelihood of local people. Soon, when the picking is all done, the olives will go in sacks to the village *eliaourgeio*, the olive press, and the long, arduous process of making the oil will begin.

Thodoros and Maria make their own wine, in *skafoni*, big barrels into which three men climb to trample the grapes, in the store room under their Liapades house. We, like creatures in a La Fontaine fable, have already eaten our 'strawberry' grapes—so black and plentiful that the vine outside the living-room window makes a deep and welcome shade in a room that once was hard to protect from the sun—and the muscats, which grow out the back and are the best of all.

This is the autumn we pray a road will finally come right down to Rovinia, at least to the top of the steps that go up by the kitchen door. Mud in winter and the heat in summer combine to make the walk through the terraces exhausting—not to mention the fact that one must go a long way round, once the olive nets are down, to avoid wrecking someone's harvest.

My clothes are packed, and Tim has set off with Thodoros, hoisting suitcases tied to the body with straps over rocky paths and through glades of orange, olive and fig. The time to leave has finally arrived. I go to the pot where I planted the mint I brought early in September, and see it has grown alongside the basil, ready to put in a drink next time we toast the setting sun at the spring equinox, as it sinks right down over the middle of the Monkey's Head.

Postscript

It's spring 2001 and I'm travelling, on a part of the island of Corfu I know so well I could spell out its twists, ruts and vertiginous turns in my sleep (so I think) and yet—dismayingly—I have no idea where I am. We have gone up to the T-junction on the road to Liapades, taken a right down past the banana yellow church and the cemetery, and passed the also-yellow post-box where no mail has been collected for seven years and my postcard to a friend in London, popped in before I knew better, has lain next to the dead of the village for all that length of time.

We've pressed on, down the steep road where houses with 'Rooms To Let'—known, surprisingly as 'Garconnieres' but with a Greek spelling and pronunciation difficult to render—each now has a Hollywood-sized pool at its back. Where, the murmur goes, do they possibly get permission for all that water? We've slowed outside Michaelis's supermarket, run by his efficient daughter Katerina, and I'm readying myself for the climb up cement steps my father installed by the side of the road over thirty years ago, before we set off across land which belongs to Michaelis, formidably fenced off and needing his key to open the lock on the gate. Then, so my inner geography insists, we cut across and back on to the path carefully laid down by my father in acceptance of the permanent non-existence of a road to the house he and my mother had built. We walk on past the house of Adonis, the Greek Canadian who has given up the donkey rides and plans to open a small shop instead. A minute later, like a flag of Greece thrown down below our rocky, boulder-strewn way—blue with the white stripes of foam that scribble the national insignia on the surface— there lies the sea. The thought of the first glimpse of the tiles on the roof of the house, rising above the expanse of unfurled blue, is what usually keeps me going, as path turns to cliffside and back again.

But not today. It's spring, and it's been raining heavily overnight, and Katerina's store is only grudgingly open, one shutter still not drawn back. Nothing new there. Only Thodoros's suddenly tense air of expectation at the wheel of my mother's little red Ford betrays the fact that we are going down to Rovinia—despite the recent rain, the threat of landslide and the knowledge that the 'new road' isn't really finished yet, on this miraculous innovation, a Road To The House.

So, instead of continuing on the road down to Yefira Bay, the Cricketers Hotel and Eli Beach Hotel, stopping to park by the side of the road under Katerina's and preparing to cart our luggage on steps, path and cliff, here we are rising steeply on a 'country road' opposite the supermarket and then turning off on to our own (shared with all those who have land either side). Wide, curving and meandering, plunging and (so it seems as Thodoros, on only his

EMMA TENNANT

second trip, takes it at a valiant speed) a rearing and gal-
loping road.

This is why I have no idea where I am—at first at least. But
once the sea flag flutters and strains in a brisk wind hundreds
of feet beneath our brave new road, of course I know where I
am. And Tim, who claims to know all along, is calling out the
landmarks as we go—'Over to the left, Dassia's daughters'
houses and the cabin just below to the right, that's where we
used to cut across past Adonis's to reach the Yefira road . . .'

There is no such thing as a free road. Thodoros's cousin
Spiro, who has made this (so it seems to us) autobahn down
through the groves to Rovinia, assures us the council will
pay for the surfacing (Rovinia has paid for Spiro's efforts, car
park carved out of the land belonging to the house, just
above the steps, and all). The Mayor of Liapades and
eight surrounding villages has given her word that the
road, termed a Fire Road for the area, will be asphalted by
the council. All we know, as we dodge a telegraph pole
the *Deii*, holy conductors of electricity, have also sworn
will be moved—and skirt a precipice on the left of this
splendid new road, this to be filled with builders' rubble as
soon as possible, to prevent a Cary Grant-on-Corniche
type accident—is that the council must move soon. Any
more heavy rain, and the wonderful new road will be
washed away entirely.

Maria is standing at the foot of our steps to greet us and
she laughs at the astonishment on our faces. For, even after
getting out of the car in the area designated for the Ford,
the tiny path leading down to the sea is as unfamiliar as a
path in a fairy-tale or a child's dream. Did we really walk

along this narrow strip of rocky *monopati* (way) with scratchy bushes and a sheer drop either side, carrying all our suitcases? And how will tourists, should they ever find the new way to Rovinia Beach, know to walk past our *Idiotikos* gate, which looks more idiotic than ever today, the gap to its side at the head of the steps wider than the gate itself? Won't they come rushing down our pebbled flight and land in their hundreds on the terrace?

There won't be any trouble for the fishermen, of course, on this road or succeeding path, which remain a right of way down to the sea. But, a short time after we've settled into the house, a day of trouble does occur—one which acts as a reminder that, however useful a road may be (no: even after the inevitable heavy rain and lack of response from the Mayor it is still not washed away) the sea is uncertain and undependable at all times.

It's a Sunday, and I'm in the sitting room on a hot, glary day, late afternoon. Most unusually, Thodoros runs into the room and dives—it's the only word for it—into the study, to use the telephone there. The extra-wide door remains open and I hear—again very unexpected—the note of panic in Thodoros's voice. It's hard for me to make out just what is wrong—then, running through the sitting room again and out to the 'prow' of the terrace, binoculars in hand, he gives a brief, breathless résumé of an impending tragedy.

Yorgos, the good-natured Liapades fisherman—who for the past thirty-five years has been as much a part of life at Rovinia as Thodoros and Maria themselves (his tread on the shingle, amplified at five each morning, has duly woken and lulled us all with its punctuality)—has failed to return from his day's outing down the coast today. As regular as the dawn departure is Yorgos's return, just before midday. He fishes, now he no longer owns a boat of his own with Theo and another Maria, the best fisherwoman in Liapades, and the trio, their voices also maximised against the sound of the waves, are as familiar as house and olive grove to us all here.

It's after five p.m. and they're not back. The sea has a southerly wind as its animator and there is a heavy swell, with fat pillows of white water pushing against the rocks. Why did they go out, in such conditions, in the first place— Yorgos and his companions, who have been fishing this stretch for at least forty years? 'To pick up the nets before it gets too rough,' Thodoros surmises. Nets are expensive; and they were left right down the coast, almost at Hermones. 'Engine may have conked out,' my mother says, as she stands a long time staring out through my father's old binoculars at the rebellious sea. 'Then, certainly, they would have gone on the rocks.'

We wait and wait and wait. Dinner—of pasta with a fresh basil sauce from the plants that grow like topiary heads in pots out on the terrace, staring in at us as we try to change the subject, and pretend we're enjoying our meal—is largely left on our plates. It's now dark. The swallows, as if sensing disaster, deliver long sermons on the perils of life at sea, from the wooden pegs driven into the wall beneath their nests. We all, gloomily, see the small boat crushed against the rocks as the scene plays again and again in our minds.

Finally, at about eleven, we go to bed. It's after midnight when I'm woken by pounding feet in the passage outside our room, and Thodoros's voice calls out—with the strength and excitement, I immediately feel, of Pythagoras's 'Eureka'—the same word: '*Evrikane!*' (They found them!) We all leap out of bed, to learn the facts: a rough sea had driven the little craft with its three fishermen into a small cove just north of Hermones, this a bay well hidden from view and explaining why Maria the fisherwoman's son hadn't spotted them on his trawl down the coast. (Though nothing can explain the discovery that in all the area, with its tourist resort of Paleocastritsa and scattered fishing communities, there is no lifeboat: when one finally did come, and find the stranded fishermen with the aid of a spotlight, it took four hours for it to come round the north of the island, all the way from Corfu town.)

It was 3 a.m. before Yorgos, Theo and Maria were brought in the rescue vessel to Paleocastritsa. We saw them on TV in black and white in the little room behind the kitchen where Maria lets some of her many grandchildren play and watch the box. Here they were, on the news: heroes of the night of near-tragedy, beaming and drinking in the presence of two hundred people, the Mayor with her Melina Mercouri looks and the chief dignitaries of the area—most importantly, the TV reporter, with his microphone.

'Oh no,' the fisherwoman Maria shouts into camera, her face alight with laughter. 'Of course we didn't starve, down there in the little bay. We had *barbounia* (red mullet) and I already had brought bread and water.'

'They had each other to keep them warm,' Yorgos put in, 'and I had no-one.'

For some days after the almost-disaster-at-sea, people made a point of visiting the cove where, it appeared, there was already a wood oven in a hole in the cliff, this used frequently by fishermen to roast or grill their catch; and jokes were made about the restaurant newly opened by—as they came to be called—the 'fab three'.

Then the talk died down, and Yorgos, who had been too busy giving press interviews in the *plateia* in Liapades to come for his usual evening drink out by the fig tree on the terrace at Rovinia, started to turn up with his wife Constantina.

Whatever may lie in store for Rovinia in the future, we all gave thanks for their safe return and pray that none of these winds carry them away from safety again: the Bora (North); the Tramontana (East; also Levantes), the Scirocco (South) or the Garbis or Pounentes or Maestro from the West.

About the Author

Emma Tennant's previous books include *Sylvia and Ted*, *The Bad Sister*, *Two Women of London*, *Faustine*, *Strangers: A Family Romance*, *Burnt Diaries* and *Pemberley*, a sequal to *Pride and Prejudice*. She lives in London.